OPPOSING VIEWPOINTS® SERIES

| Biomedical Ethics

Viqi Wagner, Book Editor

GREENHAVEN PRESS

An imprint of Thomson Gale, a part of The Thomson Corporation

THOMSON

GALE

Detroit • New York • San Francisco • New Haven, Conn. • Waterville, Maine • London

THOMSON
─────★─────™
GALE

Christine Nasso, *Publisher*
Elizabeth Des Chenes, *Managing Editor*

© 2008 The Gale Group.

Star logo is a trademark and Gale and Greenhaven Press are registered trademarks used herein under license.

For more information, contact:
Greenhaven Press
27500 Drake Rd.
Farmington Hills, MI 48331-3535
Or you can visit our Internet site at http://www.gale.com

LIBRARY OF CONGRESS CATALOGING-IN-PUBLICATION DATA

Biomedical ethics / Viqi Wagner, book editor.
    p. cm. -- (Opposing viewpoints)
    Includes bibliographical references and index.
    ISBN-13: 978-0-7377-3737-0 (hardcover)
    ISBN-13: 978-0-7377-3738-7 (pbk.)
    1. Medical ethics--Juvenile literature. I. Wagner, Viqi, 1953-
    R724.B4912 2008
    174.2--dc22
                                                    2007034362

ISBN-10: 0-7377-3737-9 (hardcover)
ISBN-10: 0-7377-3738-7 (pbk.)

Printed in the United States of America
10 9 8 7 6 5 4 3 2 1

Biomedical Ethics

Other Books of Related Interest:

"Congress shall make
no law . . . abridging
the freedom of speech,
or of the press."

First Amendment to the U.S. Constitution

The basic foundation of our democracy is the First Amendment guarantee of freedom of expression. The Opposing Viewpoints Series is dedicated to the concept of this basic freedom and the idea that it is more important to practice it than to enshrine it.

Contents

Chapter 1: Is Stem Cell Research Ethical?

Chapter 4: Is Human Genetic Testing Ethical?

Why Consider Opposing Viewpoints?

> "The only way in which a human being can make some approach to knowing the whole of a subject is by hearing what can be said about it by persons of every variety of opinion and studying all modes in which it can be looked at by every character of mind. No wise man ever acquired his wisdom in any mode but this."
>
> *John Stuart Mill*

In our media-intensive culture it is not difficult to find differing opinions. Thousands of newspapers and magazines and dozens of radio and television talk shows resound with differing points of view. The difficulty lies in deciding which opinion to agree with and which "experts" seem the most credible. The more inundated we become with differing opinions and claims, the more essential it is to hone critical reading and thinking skills to evaluate these ideas. Opposing Viewpoints books address this problem directly by presenting stimulating debates that can be used to enhance and teach these skills. The varied opinions contained in each book examine many different aspects of a single issue. While examining these conveniently edited opposing views, readers can develop critical thinking skills such as the ability to compare and contrast authors' credibility, facts, argumentation styles, use of persuasive techniques, and other stylistic tools. In short, the Opposing Viewpoints series is an ideal way to attain the higher-level thinking and reading skills so essential in a culture of diverse and contradictory opinions.

In addition to providing a tool for critical thinking, Opposing Viewpoints books challenge readers to question their own strongly held opinions and assumptions. Most people form their opinions on the basis of upbringing, peer pressure, and personal, cultural, or professional bias. By reading carefully balanced opposing views, readers must directly confront new ideas as well as the opinions of those with whom they disagree. This is not to simplistically argue that everyone who reads opposing views will—or should—change his or her opinion. Instead, the series enhances readers' understanding of their own views by encouraging confrontation with opposing ideas. Careful examination of others' views can lead to the readers' understanding of the logical inconsistencies in their own opinions, perspective on why they hold an opinion, and the consideration of the possibility that their opinion requires further evaluation.

Evaluating Other Opinions

To ensure that this type of examination occurs, Opposing Viewpoints books present all types of opinions. Prominent spokespeople on different sides of each issue as well as well-known professionals from many disciplines challenge the reader. An additional goal of the series is to provide a forum for other, less known, or even unpopular viewpoints. The opinion of an ordinary person who has had to make the decision to cut off life support from a terminally ill relative, for example, may be just as valuable and provide just as much insight as a medical ethicist's professional opinion. The editors have two additional purposes in including these less-known views. One, the editors encourage readers to respect others' opinions—even when not enhanced by professional credibility. It is only by reading or listening to and objectively evaluating others' ideas that one can determine whether they are worthy of consideration. Two, the inclusion of such viewpoints encourages the important critical thinking skill of objectively evaluating an author's credentials and bias. This evaluation will illuminate an author's reasons for taking a particular stance on an issue and will aid in readers' evaluation of the author's ideas.

It is our hope that these books will give readers a deeper understanding of the issues debated and an appreciation of the complexity of even seemingly simple issues when good and honest people disagree. This awareness is particularly important in a democratic society such as ours in which people enter into public debate to determine the common good. Those with whom one disagrees should not be regarded as enemies but rather as people whose views deserve careful examination and may shed light on one's own.

Thomas Jefferson once said that "difference of opinion leads to inquiry, and inquiry to truth." Jefferson, a broadly educated man, argued that "if a nation expects to be ignorant and free . . . it expects what never was and never will be." As individuals and as a nation, it is imperative that we consider the opinions of others and examine them with skill and discernment. The Opposing Viewpoints series is intended to help readers achieve this goal.

David L. Bender and Bruno Leone,
Founders

Introduction

"*Cases of right to life, right to die and right not to be kept alive . . . are complicated with innovations in medical science and technologies which redefine the definition of our commonly accepted concepts of life and death and transform the way we deal with them.*"

—Dame Elizabeth Butler-Sloss,
Chancellor of the University
of West England

Many debates about biomedical ethics are also debates about the definition of human life—when it starts and when it stops. Medical procedures performed on the human body between those two points are closely scrutinized because human life is valued so highly. Any scientific or medical procedure that interferes with growth of a human embryo (a fertilized ovum) or fetus (an unborn offspring) is subject to the debate about when human life begins. For example, abortion procedures and stem cell research intervene by halting further growth of an embryo or fetus. In contrast, cloning intervenes by doubling the growth of an embryo. On the other end of the spectrum, any scientific or medical procedure that interferes with a dying human body is subject to the debate about when human life ends. Assisted suicide and euthanasia intervene by ending life before the body itself shuts down. Putting a body on life support intervenes by prolonging life after the body ceases to function. Depending on when an individual believes that human life begins and ends, these procedures are seen as ethical or unethical, and each new scientific or technological development related to life's beginning and end renews these controversies. Two medical developments that illustrate debates about life and death are hormonal contraception and electroencephalography.

Hormonal contraception prevents pregnancy by acting on a woman's hormonal system to prevent fertilization of an egg or implantation of an embryo. Types of hormonal contraception include oral contraceptive pills, non-surgical devices such as the patch or vaginal ring, surgical devices such as implants, and injections such as Depo Provera. For those seeking to prevent pregnancy, the development of hormonal contraception has been very advantageous for various reasons. If used properly, hormonal contraception can be much more effective than many other forms of contraception. Additionally, because hormonal contraception does not require any specific applications or insertions during the act of intercourse, it permits spontaneous sexual relations without the fear of pregnancy. Yet those who object to hormonal contraception see these effects as dangerous disadvantages rather than benefits. Even so, those opposed to hormonal contraception may disagree about *why* it is unethical based on their respective beliefs about when human life begins.

In some instances, people object to all forms of birth control because they believe that intercourse should only occur for the purpose of generating human life. Others accept that sex can be for pleasure and bonding as well as reproduction, but object to any form of abortion. For those in the second category, the time frame in which they believe life begins is critical to their acceptance or denunciation of different forms of birth control. For some, human life begins during the process of conception when the sperm advances to fertilize the egg in a woman's womb. Since hormonal contraception can prevent conception by either stopping the ovulation of the egg or by thickening the woman's cervical mucus, thus making it more difficult for sperm to penetrate the uterus, it would be considered unethical for people in this camp because it interferes during the process when life begins.

For others, human life begins not at conception, but when the fertilized embryo begins to implant itself into the wall of the mother's womb. Therefore, forms of birth control, such as condoms, that prevent fertilization are not considered to be unethical because the process of human life has not actually started at that point. However, in addition to preventing conception, hormonal contraception can also alter a woman's endometrium, or uterine wall, making it difficult for a fertilized egg to implant and therefore survive. Those who do not object to the *contraceptive* function of hormonal treatments might seriously object to the *contragestive* function that prevents implantation. In their eyes, interfering with implantation is a form of abortion because the birth control intervenes after the implantation process when human life has begun.

Debates about when human life ends can be just as complex as those concerned with the beginning of life. One technological innovation that adds complexity to the death dilemma is electroencephalography, the measurement of the electrical activity of the brain. In contemporary medical science, doctors can use an electroencephalogram, commonly know as an EEG test, to determine brain death, or the irreversible end of all brain activity. No one was able to even comprehend the concept of brain death until medical advances during the 1960s enabled doctors to resuscitate patients after their bodies shut down and then place them on life support to keep their heart and lungs working. Bodies on life support can remain alive long after the brain ceases to function. Before life support advances, clinical death, or the end of blood circulation and respiration, was the only medical definition of death. Now, death is treated as more of a process than a particular moment in medicine.

Depending on when a person believes the actual end of life takes place in this process, certain medical procedures will be viewed either as ethical or unethical. For example, keeping a body alive after brain death long enough to extract an organ for donation may seem acceptable to some and abhorrent to others. If a person's belief system designates clinical death to be the end of life, then removing an organ after brain death is tantamount to harvesting organs from live human beings. By contrast, if brain death determines the end of a person's life, then keeping the body alive in order to preserve the healthy organ is good science.

Religions, philosophies, and value systems profess different ideas about when human life begins and ends. These differences have to be negotiated in each culture when medical and technological advances probe the mysteries of life and death. *Opposing Viewpoints: Biomedical Ethics* examines diverse arguments about contemporary hot-button issues such as stem cell research, reproductive technology, organ transplantation, and human genetic testing. These issues under contention in contemporary medical and scientific research and practices continue the process of defining and redefining human life.

OPPOSING
VIEWPOINTS®
SERIES

CHAPTER 1

Is Stem Cell Research Ethical?

Chapter Preface

Whether embryonic stem cell research is ethical is one of the most contentious debates in the early 2000s. Many people hear about stem cell research in the news media, but few know what stem cells are and how they were discovered. Research on stem cells concerns itself with finding out how an organism develops from a single cell. It also seeks to discover how healthy cells replace damaged cells in adult organisms. Knowledge about these areas can help scientists develop cell-based therapies, often referred to as regenerative or reparative treatment, that can battle diseases and heal people in ways that were thought to be impossible. However, since extracting stem cells in embryos ends the further development of the embryo, those who believe that embryos are human life find the cost of stem cell research to be too steep.

Stem cells are not like other types of cells. First, they are undifferentiated cells, or cells that do not have a special function, and they can renew themselves over and over through cell division. Second, they can develop into specialized cells such as blood, bone, brain, muscle, skin, and other cells. Under the right conditions, they can be directed to become cells that function to help beat the heart, or renew bone marrow, or produce insulin in the pancreas, to name a few possible functions. Some scientists believe that stem cells therefore may help them develop cures for diseases such as heart disease, cancer, and Parkinson's disease.

While researching a type of cancer called a teratocarcinoma in 1964, scientists noticed that a single cell could be isolated and then remain undifferentiated. Then in 1981, the first embryonic stem cells were isolated from mouse embryos. A significant breakthrough in further stem cell research happened in 1998 when scientist James Thompson and his research team at the University of Wisconsin-Madison found a way to isolate and grow stem cells from human blastocysts, or early-stage embryos.

The first human embryos used in the University of Wisconsin experiments were produced in a laboratory to help couples who had been unable to conceive babies. Several couples who were able to complete in vitro fertilization with some of their embryos gave their consent to donate the leftover embryos to science. How scientists obtain human embryos in order to study stem cells remains a major point of contention in the ethical debate. Some people fear that a demand for embryos may encourage laboratories to grow them for the sole purpose of research, in effect producing embryos with the knowledge that they will be killed in the process. In order to circumvent this hot-button issue, some stem cell scientists devote their research to finding ways to extract stem cells without causing embryos to die.

"The human embryo ... is not to be destroyed or seen as disposable tissue that can be used in research."

Embryonic Stem Cell Research Is Unethical

Thomas A. Shannon

In the following viewpoint, Thomas A. Shannon advances the religious argument that using embryonic stem cells in scientific research, even cells extracted from already destroyed human embryos, is ethically and morally unacceptable. The CatholicChurch strictly holds that the destruction of a human embryo is unethical, he maintains; by extension, there is no ethical way to use the tissues or products of stem cell research without cooperating in an immoral act. Thomas A. Shannon is a professor of religion and social ethics at Worcester Polytechnic Institute in Worcester, Massachusetts, and the author of Made in Whose Image? Genetic Engineering and Christian Ethics.

As you read, consider the following questions:

1. What is the difference between *totipotent* embryonic stem cells and *pluripotent* adult stem cells, according to Shannon?

Thomas A. Shannon, "Stem-Cell Research," *Catholic Update*, AmericanCatholic.org, January 2002. Reproduced by permission of St. Anthony Messenger Press.

2. According to Catholic teaching, when does a human organism acquire the full value and rights of a person?

3. How does the author counter the argument that a blastocyst is not yet an individual person because each cell in a blastocyst is capable of developing into a whole human being?

Over the last two decades scientific developments have been proceeding at a rapid pace. Nowhere has this been more true than in human genetics. One cannot pick up the daily paper or listen to a news show without hearing of yet another new discovery, development or application of a new procedure.

There are two main problems with this steady stream of information: The information itself is becoming more and more complex and the applications are predicted to be revolutionary. Frequently the research is only at the very beginning stages. Much of this research has an ethical dimension. In this [viewpoint] we'll take a look at the field of stem-cell research. We'll explain what stem cells are and why there are ethical concerns.

Most Americans have had some sort of a biology course in high school; some have had a college-level course; but few have had specific courses in molecular genetics or bioengineering. Thus we may have some sort of general idea of the topic, but not grasp the real core issues. Several ethical issues were raised with the recent near-completion of the Human Genome Project (the project that identified and mapped the structure of human DNA)—privacy, potential disqualification for insurance, the possibility of predicting some aspects of one's health at birth, to name just a few. The technology goes forward, however, and often without sufficient breathing room to understand the technology, much less consider its implications.

Research on adult and embryonic stem cells of animals and humans has been going on for several years, and a national bioethics commission made some recommendations about this research. On August 9, 2001, President Bush announced his decision to allow the federal government to provide funding for research on 64 lines of embryonic stem cells. These lines came from destroyed human embryos obtained from in vitro fertilization clinics. The president's decision caused an enormous debate in terms of both science and ethics. Many commentators, religious leaders, scientists and members of the public weighed in on various sides of the debate, and an advisory committee will now [as of 2002] monitor the research. But what is the debate about?

What Are Stem Cells, Anyway?

First, what are stem cells and why are they so important? Essentially, stem cells are cells that have the potential to become many different kinds of cells. They are the means by which cells in the body can be replenished. In the very early embryo these cells are *totipotent*—that is, they have the potency to become any kind of body cell. In adult stem cells, the cells are *pluripotent*—they have the capacity to become a variety of cells, but not all. Scientists hope to obtain lines of these embryonic stem cells—large numbers of them grown from a common source—and coax them into becoming specific kinds of cells.

For example, a biologist at my college recently succeeded in having blood cells from bone marrow grow into nerve cells. Other scientists have recently reported success in having embryonic stem cells grow into three different types of blood cells. The goal of this research is to use these stem cells to develop various tissues that can then be used to repair damaged tissues in the body—heart tissue to repair a damaged heart, nerve tissue to repair a damaged spinal column or reverse the effects of Alzheimer's disease. The research is very interesting, complex and promising.

Which Stem Cells?

Now let's look at a particular kind of ethical problem. Which stem cells should be used for research, adult or embryonic? Many have argued that adult stem cells are difficult to obtain, very hard to coax into developing into other tissues and, consequently, their use would involve much more time and money to obtain the desired results. Up until very recently, this was generally true.

But now [2002] research has shown that adult stem cells can be isolated and developed. If this research continues to be successful, there may [be] no reason whatsoever to use embryonic stem cells, which requires destruction of early embryos and poses a serious ethical problem. Many argue that adult stem cells are where the resources for stem-cell research should be directed. Continued success in this area would essentially eliminate the need for embryonic stem cells—and put an end to a major ethical problem.

But the problem is that the Bush proposal—and indeed the desire of many scientists and many in Congress—is to use federal funds to support research on stem cells extracted from *already destroyed* human embryos. Is this ethical? There are actually two ethical questions here: First, is the destruction of the very early embryo immoral? Second, if a vaccine or tissue is generated from these human embryonic stem cells, would someone act unethically in using it?

Over the last few decades there has been a strong affirmation by the pope and bishops that the human embryo is to be valued and, in effect, treated as a person from the time of fertilization forward. It is not to be destroyed or seen as disposable tissue that can be used in research as any other tissue might be. Nor should such embryos be generated specifically for research purposes. This of course is possible, given the technology of in vitro, "outside the body," fertilization. And in fact, one fertility clinic in Virginia has reported that in fact that is exactly what it is doing.

Reactions from Pope and Bishops

What is the moral status of the early embryo? Pope John Paul II gave his perspective on this debate in an address to President Bush on July 23, 2001, during his papal visit. The pope rearticulated his position on the use of embryos by saying:

> Experience is already showing how a tragic coarsening of consciences accompanies the assault on innocent human life in the womb, leading to accommodation and acquiescence in the face of other related evils such as euthanasia, infanticide and, most recently, proposals for the creation for research purposes of human embryos, destined to be destroyed in the process.

The pope also called for the United States to show the world that we can be masters and not products of technology.

In a similar, though more specific response to the Bush stem-cell proposal, Bishop Joseph A. Fiorenza, then president of the U.S. Conference of Catholic Bishops, said:

> However, the trade-off [Bush] has announced is morally unacceptable: The federal government, for the first time in history, will support research that relies on the destruction of some defenseless human beings for the possible benefit to others. However such a decision is hedged about with qualification, it allows our nation's research enterprise to cultivate a disrespect for human life. . . . The President's policy may therefore prove to be as unworkable as it is morally wrong, ultimately serving only those whose goal is unlimited embryo research.

These claims are reflective of the traditional teaching recently restated, for example, in the Instruction from the Congregation for the Doctrine of the Faith, *Donum Vitae*, that the

Today, Embryonic Stem Cell Research. Tomorrow, Eugenics

The alternative of adult stem cells is greatly needed in a scientific community willing to go to nearly any length for medical advancement. The use of the human embryo as a source of stem cells holds terrible ramifications, because the process of removing stem cells destroys the embryo. While scientists try to justify their research with the notion that embryos are not yet human life, many ethicists dismiss this idea for what it clearly is—a lie, a feeble attempt to rationalize their experiments. . . .

Many remain undecided about the status of the embryo. Hilde Lindemann Nelson, Ph.D., associate professor of philosophy at Michigan State University, says, "I don't think there is an easy answer to what we do with these embryos because we don't yet have any common standing on what kind of moral status they have." Former President Ronald Reagan once stated, "If there's doubt about it, and if there's mystery, then shouldn't we be extraordinarily careful?" The smallest possibility of destroying a human life should rule out this research. Science should never advance by sacrificing the very lives it should be trying to save.

Author of *Culture of Death: The Assault on Medical Ethics in America* Wesley J. Smith asks, "Once embryos can be exploited for their stem cells to promote human welfare, what is to stop scientists from manipulating embryos to control and direct human evolution—equally for the purpose of improving the human future?" He notes that many of those who signed a letter to President [George W.] Bush urging an end to the ban on federal funding for human embryo research were scientists and bioethicists favoring eugenics, [intervention to improve or select hereditary traits] a movement that ignores the sanctity of human life. . . .

[Christian writer and medieval scholar] C. S. Lewis emphasized these dangers when he wrote, "If any age really attains, by eugenics and scientific education, the power to make its descendants what it pleases, all men who live after are the patients of that power," slaves to the "dead hand of the great planners and conditioners."

Frighteningly, the 21st century appears to be that age, and scientists may enter this era through the backing of a society that allows them to devalue human life at its earliest and most vulnerable stage.

Stephanie Porowski and Emma Elliott, "Adult Stem-Cell Treatments: A Better Way," Concerned Women for America, *December 1, 2005.*

"human being is to be respected and treated as a person from the moment of conception and therefore from that same moment his rights as a person must be recognized."

The Instruction is careful to note that the Church has not taken a philosophical position on the time of ensoulment. However, "From the moment of conception, the life of every human being is to be respected in an absolute way . . ." (*Donum Vitae*, Introduction).

While the hierarchy of the Catholic Church has left open the resolution of the actual time of ensoulment, it has in fact insisted that the prudent response would be to recognize that as a practical matter ensoulment is coincident with fertilization. This position, combined with the traditional respect-for-life position of the Church, is what propels its opposition to embryonic stem-cell research.

The Beginning of Life

Some, while respecting this teaching of the Church, make further ethical observations about the early embryo. First, fertilization is a process that takes about 24 hours to complete and therefore is not a specific moment one can point to. As a side note, should a human be cloned, there would be no fertilization at all because the nucleus of one cell is placed into another cell that has its nucleus removed and is stimulated to begin cell division. The life of that individual would not begin at fertilization.

Second, the whole development of an embryo into a fetus and eventually into a child is a process, not a series of sharply defined steps. This is important because it is really difficult to tell precisely where a fetus is in the process of development. One knows where the fetus is after the stage has been entered into. It is not easy to make precise developmental statements and then moral judgments made in relation to them.

But more specifically, many ethicists focus on the fact that up until about a week or so into the pregnancy, the fertilized egg has the capacity to divide and become identical twins. In some cases it has been observed that such divided eggs blend back together into one blastocyst (what the fertilized egg is called at around 4–5 days of development).

And if the egg is fertilized in vitro, one cell can be removed (to have its genetic structure analyzed) and the developmental process is not harmed. In fact, all the cells of the blastocyst can be separated and each has the capacity to become a whole human being. This point is clearly important biologically: These cells can become either a whole organism or be coaxed into becoming any specialized cell in the body.

But this is important philosophically also. Because the cells of the blastocyst can be divided so that each part can become a whole, the blastocyst lacks true individuality—the capacity not to be able to be divided.

If one were to divide me, you would wind up with two halves. If one divides the cells of the blastocyst, one obtains several cells all capable of becoming individuals. The reason why this is philosophically important is that if the organism is not first an individual, it is difficult to understand how it could be a person. Being an individual organism is a first necessary, though certainly not sufficient, stage for being a person.

On the basis of the argument that the blastocyst is not yet an individual, some would argue that while the blastocyst is a living organism, possessing the human genetic code, such an organism is indeed valuable, but its value is not yet that accorded to a person.

Therefore some would conclude that killing the human blastocyst is not murder because there is as yet no personal subject to experience that wrong. Such a killing is a disvalue, to be sure, but a disvalue that might be offset by other positive values, such as health. The conclusion that some would draw, then, is that at least a case can be made for the use of human embryos in stem-cell research.

Once again, the Church does not endorse this view. The specific reason for the rejection of this position is the affirmation that fertilization, the time when egg and sperm merge and form a new genotype, is considered to be the biological beginning of the new human life. Together with this affirmation is the correlative presumption that this is the time of the infusion of the soul. Although there is no official doctrine on this position, the attitude of the Church is that moral priority should be given to this position.

The second problem is, could someone use a vaccine or tissues from such research in an ethical way? The term for this problem in moral theology is called *cooperation*. It can be either *formal* or *material*. Formal cooperation involves a person directly intending to participate in the evil act of another. For example, a person would be formally cooperating with a moral wrong if he or she obtained drugs and helped prepare them so they can be used for euthanasia.

Cooperation may be material, not formal, if a person does not intend the evil act but may be involved in some of its consequences. For example, a nurse who is opposed to abortion but works in a hospital where abortions are occasionally performed may still provide nursing care for the woman who came for abortion.

In the case of stem-cell research, this framework of degrees of cooperation allows several responses to be proposed. First, the patient need not intend the destruction of the embryos and thus any cooperation would not be formal. Thus, one could use the vaccines without an ethical breach. Second, the moral distance between the use of the vaccine by the patient and the original research is so great as to render any cooperation remote at best.

Finally, for use of the research to be immoral, the act of destroying a blastocyst must itself be immoral. If one follows the line of reasoning that the blastocyst is not yet an individual and, therefore, not yet a person, its killing would certainly be a disvalue but would not be a moral evil having the equivalence of murder. Thus individuals would be able to use the clinical products that come from such research.

Such reasoning would be unacceptable to the teaching of, for example, *Donum Vitae* or the encyclical letter of John Paul II *Evangelium Vitae*. The basis for rejecting such procedures is the recognition of the human embryo's being accepted as a full human person from the moment of conception and, therefore, having an intrinsic dignity and value that cannot be compromised in the name of other values.

The Broader Ethical Question

But there is another question that is, I think, equally as important as the ethics of the use of human embryos in research. That question is a public policy question: Should we continue with our policy of research into high-tech, expensive therapies that may not be available to many citizens because they are uninsured, underinsured, or because their insurance plans might not cover experimental treatments? The dominant trend in American medicine is high-tech intervention to cure or try to maintain the status quo of a patient. The implantation of a new model of an artificial heart is another example of such high-tech intervention. Clearly many of these interventions do save lives. And significant developments have been made in the treatment of many forms of cancer. But some perceptions of the success of these interventions are inflated. One study showed that on television shows the success rate of cardiopulmonary resuscitation is over 70%. In real hospitals, however, the success rate is under 5%. This is not in itself a reason not to do CPR, but perhaps we might question whether it is appropriate in the particular circumstances of this patient.

The stem-cell debate might be an opportunity for us to ask if we should not, as a nation, begin to focus on prevention rather than cure as our dominant health-care strategy.

Prevention will not prevent all diseases and will not help if there is a trauma such as a car accident. But a strategy of prevention including services such as care for pregnant women including proper diet information, well-baby exams including vaccinations, and information on lifestyle issues such as diet, smoking and excess drinking would go a long way to preventing the early onset of many diseases.

The resistance to removing or restricting the use of soda and candy machines in elementary and secondary schools shows that we have a long way to go in even thinking about the most elemental forms of prevention of disease.

Of course prevention is rather boring. It certainly would make for very dull TV shows. Who would not rather watch the fast-paced, high-tech ER than a physician instruct a person in a proper diet? Anyway, who wants to watch his or her diet all the time? Who has time for exercise and all the other things we learn are good for us? Prevention is a hard sell. But, in the long run, it is better to try to prevent heart disease than repair a damaged heart. It is better to manage one's diet than take insulin continuously or have a leg amputated because of circulation problems resulting from diabetes.

Spending Carefully

I am not arguing that we should abandon research or high-tech medicine. I am arguing that we as a country seriously need a national debate on health care and the kind of interventions that would be beneficial for all citizens, not just the wealthy.

Currently, it seems like much research on specific diseases is driven by powerful lobbying groups who have celebrity spokespersons who sometimes have the disease for which funding is sought. Parents whose children are afflicted with terrible diseases bring their children to congressional hearing rooms. The implication is that if Congress does not fund this particular legislation and a relative dies, it is the direct fault of

Congress. But we know that we cannot fund research for all diseases, and certainly we cannot fund them equally. While all of us are sympathetic to the plight of the sick and suffering, a genuine ethical question is, who get access to such congressional hearings? One seldom sees the poor, the socially marginalized, the unemployed, the underinsured moving about in these circles. How does health-care policy affect their lives, particularly since they probably have no insurance to begin with?

What I am arguing here is that the stem-cell debate focuses our attention on yet another critical and important technical development in the fight against disease. Yet it also should make us question whether we as a country should channel all our resources to this form of research, or should we also begin to devote resources to prevention. Our health-care budget is limited; thus the question of the justice of how such resources are allocated is a critical one.

In addressing all of the questions covered in this update, it's important to remember the Church does not wish merely to be a naysayer against development and scientific progress. In fact, the Church is very positive and supportive about advances in science that improve the quality of human life.

Most of the world knows that the Church works in many places, often in areas of high poverty, seeking to help liberate the human family from disease. In evaluating how to move ahead, whether it is in the laboratory or in society at large, always we are to remember an underlying principle: to value the dignity of human life.

"An embryo is no more a human person than an acorn is an oak tree."

Embryonic Stem Cell Research Is Ethical

Ronald A. Lindsay

There is no evidence, or persuasive argument, that the use of embryos in stem cell research amounts to killing an individual human person, Ronald A. Lindsay maintains in the following viewpoint. Individual identity is a necessary condition for possessing moral rights, Lindsay argues, and a five-day embryo has no individual identity—it is a mere group of undifferentiated cells that might divide and develop separately, and it has no consciousness, experience, senses, or any other quality associated with whole human persons. He concludes that the potential of an embryo to contribute to life-saving medical therapy is far greater than its intrinsic potential to become a person, and therefore there is a moral imperative to allow embryonic stem cell research. Ronald A. Lindsay is legal director of the Center for Inquiry, an international nonprofit organization committed to ethical scientific inquiry and rational, secular alternatives to paranormal and religious beliefs.

Ronald A. Lindsay, "Stem Cell Research: An Approach to Bioethics Based on Scientific Naturalism," *A White Paper from the Center for Inquiry, Office of Public Policy*, July 26, 2006. Reproduced by permission.

As you read, consider the following questions:

1. Why are fetal and adult stem cells inferior to embryonic stem cells in research, according to Lindsay?

2. How does the phenomenon of twinning show that an embryo is not an individual and there is no single moment of conception, in the author's opinion?

3. Why do the embryos researchers propose to use already have "absolutely no chance of developing into a human person," according to the author?

In vetoing the [2006] legislation that would have permitted funding of research carried out on a limited class of embryonic stem cells, namely those derived from spare embryos generated through in vitro fertilization (IVF) procedures, President [George W.] Bush characterized embryonic stem cell research as "the taking of innocent human life" and asserted that each embryo "is a unique human life with inherent dignity and matchless value."

If human embryos are entitled to the full protection of our moral norms and the use of such embryos in research is equivalent to murder, then opposition to such research is understandable. However, we should not simply assume, without benefit of a well-reasoned and persuasive argument, that our moral norms and principles apply to embryos. . . .

We conclude that no such argument has been advanced. Furthermore, the view that use of embryos in research is equivalent to the unjustified killing of human persons is inconsistent with accepted scientific evidence, in particular evidence regarding embryonic development, and is not supported by a coherent moral theory. Given the immense benefits that we might derive from embryonic stem cell research, including the development of therapies that could ameliorate or eliminate many debilitating and disabling illnesses and injuries, not only is government funding of such research permissible, but government support of such research furthers critical interests of our society and is of paramount importance. . . .

Different Kinds of Stem Cells Have Different Potential

Stem cells are present in all stages of an organism, including the embryonic, fetal and adult stages.

However, embryonic stem cells have properties that are different from fetal or adult stem cells. In the early embryo (to around the five-day stage), each cell is totipotent, that is, under the appropriate conditions each cell could develop into a complete, individual organism. After five days, the embryo becomes a blastocyst, consisting of an outer sphere that can develop into membranes such as the placenta and an inner cell mass that can develop into a fetus. The cells of the inner mass are pluripotent, meaning they develop into any cell type in the body, but they are no longer totipotent. Embryonic stem cells from the inner mass of the blastocyst stage are currently the primary source of stem cells for research. One reason they are used in research is that they are considered to be more promising for work on most research projects than fetal stem cells and adult stem cells.

One problem with adult stem cells is that they do not appear to have the same potential to proliferate under research conditions as embryonic stem cells. Embryonic stem cells can proliferate for a year or more in the laboratory without differentiating, but to date scientists have been unsuccessful in obtaining similar results with adult stem cells. Moreover, adult stem cells are, at best, multipotent or multisomatic rather than pluripotent. Finally, and most importantly, it is still unclear whether true transdifferentiation can occur with adult stem cells, that is, it is unclear whether adult stem cells have the ability to develop into many different types of tissue as opposed to developing into different types of cells of similar

35

tissue. For example, bone marrow stem cells can give rise to bone cells and other types of connective tissue, but do not appear capable of differentiating into other sorts of tissue.

Fetal stem cells appear to have pluripotent capacities, but these cells are at a later stage of development, which creates difficulties in using them for research. Moreover, there are ethical objections to using fetal stem cells in research as well, so it is doubtful whether there is any advantage to using them in research instead of embryonic stem cells. . . .

The Moral Benefits of Embryonic Stem Cell Research

The intense interest in stem cell research reflects the potential for developing important, indeed revolutionary, therapies as a result of this research. If stem cells can be reliably directed to differentiate into specific cell types, there is the possibility of developing replacement tissues for millions of Americans who suffer from debilitating diseases and disabilities, including Parkinson's and Alzheimer's diseases, diabetes, heart disease, liver disease, and spinal cord injury, to name just a few. Although there is no certainty that such therapies could be developed, the research to date appears promising. For example, dopamine-producing neurons generated from mouse embryonic stem cells have proved functional in animals, thus indicating there is a realistic possibility that similar results could be reproduced in humans, with beneficial consequences to those suffering from Parkinson's. Even more dramatic results were obtained recently via an experiment conducted by researchers at Johns Hopkins University. These researchers were able to use neurons derived from embryonic stem cells to restore motor function in paralyzed rats.

The moral imperative to pursue research with such potentially beneficial consequences seems clear. Alleviation of suffering and restoration of health are important goals even if only one individual is benefited. If millions of individuals may

Embryo Is to Human as Acorn Is to Tree

Consider an analogy: although every oak tree was once an acorn, it does not follow that acorns are oak trees, or that I should treat the loss of an acorn eaten by a squirrel in my front yard as the same kind of loss as the death of an oak tree felled by a storm. Despite their developmental continuity, acorns and oak trees differ. So do human embryos and human beings, and in the same way. Just as acorns are potential oaks, human embryos are potential human beings.

The distinction between a potential person and an actual one makes a moral difference. Sentient creatures make claims on us that nonsentient ones do not; beings capable of experience and consciousness make higher claims still. Human life develops by degrees.

Michael J. Sandel, "Embryo Ethics." The Boston Globe, April 8, 2007. www.boston.com/news/globe.

be benefited, stem cell research assumes critical importance and warrants substantial support from federal funding.

The Early Embryo Is Not an Individual

However, there are some who believe that embryos deserve the full range of rights provided to human persons and that removing from an embryo that possibility of developing the capacities and properties characteristic of human persons is morally equivalent to killing an adult human. Those who hold this view maintain we should not "harm" embryos by utilizing them in stem cell research, just as we do not kill adult humans for research purposes.

An essential premise of this position is that even though the embryo does not currently possess the capacities and properties of human persons, it possesses the potential to develop these capacities and properties, and this potential is sufficient to provide it with the moral status of a human person. On this view, an embryo is merely a human person at an early stage of development. Another essential premise of this position—but one that is not always acknowledged—is that the embryo is already an individual. A necessary condition for possessing moral rights is individual identity. As the President's Council on Bioethics recognizes, "individuality is essential to human personhood and capacity for moral status." We do not grant moral rights to mere groupings of cells, even if they are genetically unique. . . .

Until gastrulation [when the precursor to the spinal cord appears, in the third week of development], an embryo can divide into two or more parts, each of which, given appropriate conditions, might develop into separate human beings. This is the phenomenon known as "twinning" (although division into three or four separate parts is also possible). The phenomenon of twinning establishes that there is not one determinate individual from the moment of conception; adult humans are *not* numerically identical with a previously existing zygote or embryo, if that were true, then each of a pair of twins would be numerically identical with the same embryo. This is a logically incoherent position. If A and B are separate individuals, they cannot both be identical with a previously existing entity, C.

Many of those who contend that embryos are entitled to the same rights as human persons are aware of the twinning phenomenon but they discount its significance. First, they maintain that this phenomenon does not affect those embryos that do not separate. Second, even for those embryos that undergo twinning, they maintain that this process does not undermine the claim that there was at least one individual from the moment of conception. In the words of the 2002 majority report of the President's Council on Bioethics: "The fact that where 'John' alone once was there are now both 'John' and 'Jim' does not call into question the presence of 'John' at the outset."

This reasoning is unpersuasive. Addressing first the situation where twinning does occur, if "John" was there from the beginning and "Jim" originated later, this implies that at least some twins (and triplets, etc.) have different points of origin. This anomaly creates insuperable difficulties for a view that insists all human persons come into existence at the moment of conception. Are some twins not human?

More importantly, the assertion that "John" is present from the outset—that is, there is at least one individual present from the moment of conception—is nothing more than a dogmatic claim masquerading as scientific fact. There is no scientific evidence to establish the presence of a "John." What the science of embryonic development shows is that the early embryo consists of a grouping of cells with a genetic composition similar to the genetic composition of adult humans and that, after a period of time, these cells begin to differentiate and to organize themselves into a unified organism. Prior to gastrulation, there is no certainty that these cells will differentiate and organize nor is there any certainty that these cells will become one, two or more individuals. In the words of the Human Embryo Research Panel, the cells of an early embryo do not form part "of a coherent, organized, individual." The phenomenon of twinning confirms that the early embryo is not a unified, organized, determinate individual. To insist otherwise is to maintain—without any supporting evidence—that there must be some occult organizing principles which we have not yet been able to detect. Effectively, the position that there simply must be a determinate individual from the moment of conception is a restatement of ancient ensoulment views in modern dress.

The "Potential" of the Embryo Does Not Make It a Human Person

The fact that the early embryo is not an individual has obvious implications for the argument that the embryo is entitled to protection because it possesses the potential to develop capacities and properties characteristic of human persons. We cannot refer meaningfully to the potential of the embryo if it is not yet an individual.

However, even leaving the phenomenon of twinning aside, the argument from the potential of the embryo is not cogent for several reasons. The possibility that an embryo might develop into a human person does not obviate the fact that it has not yet acquired the capacities and properties of a person. An embryo is no more a human person than an acorn is an oak tree. Not only do embryos lack consciousness and awareness, but they do not have experiences of any kind, even of the most rudimentary sort. As already indicated, they have not even undergone cell differentiation.

Those who oppose embryonic research often try to minimize the gap between potential and actual possession of the characteristics of a human person by suggesting that the embryo's path of development is inevitable. They assert that the embryo has the same genetic composition as the human person it will become and these genes provide it with the intrinsic capability of developing into that human person. But this suggestion overlooks the important role that extrinsic conditions play in embryonic and fetal development. Those who claim full moral status for the embryo seem to regard gestation within a woman's uterus as an inconsequential and incidental detail. Obviously, it is not. The embryo must be provided with the appropriate conditions for development to occur. The embryo does not have the capability of expressing its "potential" on its own.

Recognition of this fact has special relevance in the context of the debate over stem cell research because of the two possible sources of embryonic stem cells, namely spare embryos from IVF [in vitro fertilization] procedures and embryos created from SCNT [somatic cell nuclear transfer, which does not involve sperm-egg fertilization]. In neither case are the embryos being removed from conditions that might permit their development. The spare embryos from IVF procedures have not been and will not be implanted in a uterus; instead, they will either be stored for an indefinite period or discarded. Therefore, they have no prospect of developing into a human person. Their potential is no more than a theoretical construct.

The lack of any real potential to develop into a human person is even clearer in the case of embryos that might be created through SCNT. These embryos will be created with the specific intention of being used solely for research. Therefore, unless they are misappropriated by some pro-embryo activist and covertly, implanted in a uterus they have absolutely no chance of developing into a human person. It is misleading to speak of the potential of embryos to become human persons when the likelihood of such an event approaches zero.

Furthermore, the creation of embryos through SCNT shows that the argument from potential proves too much. Through SCNT, a somatic cell is allowed to express its potential to be transformed into an embryo that is latent in its genes but has been suppressed. If gene-based potential to develop into a human person is sufficient to provide an entity with full moral status, then each somatic cell in a human person's body has the same moral status as the person herself. This conclusion ... would make even standard organ donation morally unacceptable.

The conclusion that all the cells in a person's body possess the same moral rights as the person herself is just one of the unacceptable conclusions that follow from granting embryos the status of human persons. These unacceptable consequences

| *"Some people argue that finding new cures for disease requires the destruction of human embryos. . . . I disagree."*

The Development of New Stem Cell Lines Is Unethical

George W. Bush

In August 2001, U.S. president George W. Bush announced that federal funding for embryonic stem cell research would be limited to research involving stem cell lines already in existence, for which he argued the "life-and-death decision" to destroy embryos had already been made. He adhered to his no-new-stem-cell-lines policy in July 2006, when he issued the first veto of his presidency against H.R. 810, a bill calling for federal funding of research using surplus embryos (which would otherwise be discarded) donated by fertility clinic patients (with their written consent). In the following viewpoint, Bush reiterates his position that destroying embryos to develop new stem cell lines is an immoral and unethical destruction of human life, justifies his veto of H.R. 810, and argues that by using only preexisting stem cell lines, important research is going forward in an ethical way.

George W. Bush, "President Discusses Stem Cell Research Policy," East Room address, White House Office of the Press Secretary, July 19, 2006.

As you read, consider the following questions:

1. According to Bush, why did he sign S. 3504 into law but veto H.R. 810?

2. What evidence does Bush offer to show that researchers are satisfied with preexisting stem cell lines?

3. What new directions of stem cell research does the president consider morally acceptable?

Congress has just [on July 19, 2006] passed and sent to my desk two bills concerning the use of stem cells in biomedical research. These bills illustrate both the promise and perils we face in the age of biotechnology. In this new era, our challenge is to harness the power of science to ease human suffering without sanctioning the practices that violate the dignity of human life.

In 2001, I spoke to the American people and set forth a new policy on stem cell research that struck a balance between the needs of science and the demands of conscience. When I took office, there was no federal funding for human embryonic stem cell research. Under the policy I announced five years ago, my administration became the first to make federal funds available for this research, yet only on embryonic stem cell lines derived from embryos that had already been destroyed.

Embryos Must Not Be Destroyed in the Name of Research

My administration has made available more than $90 million for research on these lines. This policy has allowed important research to go forward without using taxpayer funds to encourage the further deliberate destruction of human embryos.

One of the bills Congress has passed [S. 3504] builds on the progress we have made over the last five years. So I signed it into law. Congress has also passed a second bill [H.R. 810]

Biomedical Research Can Advance Without Killing Embryos

We desire to see biomedical science advance towards therapies and cures for diseases. Our objection is not to embryonic stem cell research as such, but to the killing of embryonic human beings to harvest their stem cells. We support research using stem cells that can be obtained harmlessly from bone marrow, fat, and other non-embryonic sources. The day may well come—and come soon—when it is possible to obtain embryonic stem cells without killing embryos. It is likely that at some point in the future scientists will be able to reprogram adult cells back to the embryonic stage. Even sooner, it may be possible to create non-embryonic entities . . . from which embryonic-type stem cells may be obtained. When that day comes, we will enthusiastically support research using these cells. Now and always, though, we believe that biomedical science must remain faithful to the moral norm against killing in the cause of healing. To fail in fidelity to this norm is to undermine the moral foundations of the very enterprise of biomedical science. We must not allow our desire for scientific advancements, and even for therapies and cures, to cloud our judgments as to what human embryos are and what it means for us deliberately to kill them.

Robert P. George and Patrick Lee, "Acorns and Embryos,"
New Atlantis, *no. 7, Fall 2004/Winter 2005.*

that attempts to overturn the balanced policy I set. This bill would support the taking of innocent human life in the hope of finding medical benefits for others. It crosses a moral boundary that our decent society needs to respect, so I vetoed it.

Like all Americans, I believe our nation must vigorously pursue the tremendous possibility that science offers to cure disease and improve the lives of millions. We have opportunities to discover cures and treatments that were unthinkable generations ago. Some scientists believe that one source of these cures might be embryonic stem cell research. Embryonic stem cells have the ability to grow into specialized adult tissues, and this may give them the potential to replace damaged or defective cells or body parts and treat a variety or diseases.

Yet we must also remember that embryonic stem cells come from human embryos that are destroyed for their cells. Each of these human embryos is a unique human life with inherent dignity and matchless value. We see that value in the children [invited to appear with the president.] Each of these children began his or her life as a frozen embryo that was created for in vitro fertilization, but remained unused after the fertility treatments were complete. Each of these children was adopted while still an embryo, and has been blessed with the chance to grow up in a loving family.

These boys and girls are not spare parts. They remind us of what is lost when embryos are destroyed in the name of research. They remind us that we all begin our lives as a small collection of cells. And they remind us that in our zeal for new treatments and cures, America must never abandon our fundamental morals.

Scientific Breakthroughs Are Possible Without Destroying Embryos

Some people argue that finding new cures for disease requires the destruction of human embryos like the ones that these families adopted. I disagree. I believe that with the right techniques and the right policies, we can achieve scientific progress while living up to our ethical responsibilities. That's what I sought in 2001, when I set forth my administration's policy allowing federal funding for research on embryonic stem cell lines where the life and death decision had already been made.

This balanced approach has worked. Under this policy, 21 human embryonic stem cell lines are currently in use in research that is eligible for federal funding. Each of these lines can be replicated many times. And as a result, the National Institutes of Health have helped make more than 700 shipments to researchers since 2001. There is no ban on embryonic stem cell research. To the contrary, even critics of my policy concede that these federally funded lines are being used in research every day by scientists around the world. My policy has allowed us to explore the potential of embryonic stem cells, and it has allowed America to continue to lead the world in this area.

Since I announced my policy in 2001, advances in scientific research have also shown the great potential of stem cells that are derived without harming human embryos. My administration has expanded the funding of research into stem cells that can be drawn from children, adults, and the blood in umbilical cords, with no harm to the donor. And these stem cells are already being used in medical treatments. . . .

They are living proof that effective medical science can also be ethical. Researchers are now also investigating new techniques that could allow doctors and scientists to produce stem cells just as versatile as those derived from human embryos. One technique scientists are exploring would involve reprogramming an adult cell. For example, a skin cell to function like an embryonic stem cell. Science offers the hope that we may one day enjoy the potential benefits of embryonic stem cells without destroying human life.

We must continue to explore these hopeful alternatives and advance the cause of scientific research while staying true to the ideals of a decent and humane society. [S. 3504] prohibits one of the most egregious abuses in biomedical research, the trafficking in human fetuses that are created with the sole intent of aborting them to harvest their parts. [S. 3504 also bans trafficking in stem cells gestated for research purposes.] Human beings are not a raw material to be exploited, or a commodity to be bought or sold, and this bill will help ensure that we respect the fundamental ethical line.

I'm disappointed that Congress failed to pass another bill that would have promoted good research. . . . It would have authorized additional federal funding for promising new research that could produce cells with the abilities of embryonic cells, but without the destruction of human embryos. This is an important piece of legislation. This bill was unanimously approved by the Senate; it received 273 votes in the House of Representatives, but was blocked by a minority in the House using procedural maneuvers. I'm disappointed that the House failed to authorize funding for this vital and ethical research.

It makes no sense to say that you're in favor of finding cures for terrible diseases as quickly as possible, and then block a bill that would authorize funding for promising and ethical stem cell research. At a moment when ethical alternatives are becoming available, we cannot lose the opportunity to conduct research that would give hope to those suffering from terrible diseases and help move our nation beyond the current controversies over embryonic stem cell research.

We must pursue this research. And so I direct the Secretary of Health and Human Services, Secretary Leavitt, and the Director of the National Institutes of Health to use all the tools at their disposal to aid the search for stem cell techniques that advance promising medical science in an ethical and morally responsible way.

Unfortunately, Congress has sent me a bill that fails to meet this ethical test. This legislation [H.R. 810] would overturn the balanced policy on embryonic stem cell research that my administration has followed for the past five years. This bill would also undermine the principle that Congress, itself, has followed for more than a decade, when it has prohibited federal funding for research that destroys human embryos.

If this bill would have become law, American taxpayers would, for the first time in our history, be compelled to fund the deliberate destruction of human embryos. And I'm not going to allow it.

Holding a Moral Line on Behalf of the American People

I made it clear to the Congress that I will not allow our nation to cross this moral line. I felt like crossing this line would be a mistake, and once crossed, we would find it almost impossible to turn back. Crossing the line would needlessly encourage a conflict between science and ethics that can only do damage to both, and to our nation as a whole. If we're to find the right ways to advance ethical medical research, we must also be willing, when necessary, to reject the wrong ways. So today, I'm keeping the promise I made to the American people by returning this bill to Congress with my veto.

As science brings us ever closer to unlocking the secrets of human biology, it also offers temptations to manipulate human life and violate human dignity. Our conscience and history as a nation demand that we resist this temptation. America was founded on the principle that we are all created equal, and endowed by our Creator with the right to life. We can advance the cause of science while upholding this founding promise. We can harness the promise of technology without becoming slaves to technology. And we can ensure that science serves the cause of humanity instead of the other way around.

America pursues medical advances in the name of life, and we will achieve the great breakthroughs we all seek with reverence for the gift of life. I believe America's scientists have the ingenuity and skill to meet this challenge. And I look forward to working with Congress and the scientific community to achieve these great and noble goals in the years ahead.

> *"There are 400,000 frozen embryos in the United States, and a large percentage of those are going to be thrown out. . . . It's a better moral decision to use them to help people."*

The Development of New Stem Cell Lines Is Ethical

James Thomson, interviewed by Alan Boyle

In 1998 American developmental biologist and veterinarian James Thomson and his colleagues at the University of Wisconsin at Madison made history by deriving the first embryonic stem cell lines from frozen human embryos. In the following viewpoint, Thomson, interviewed by MSNBC science editor Alan Boyle, argues that those original stem cell lines now have limited value: Researchers have learned how to make better cell lines for basic research and for the clinical therapies Thomson predicts will be available within ten years. Developing new stem cell lines using embryos that are only going to be discarded anyway is ethically sound to Thomson, and in his view, is the only way to produce safe, effective treatments.

As you read, consider the following questions:

1. How are new embryonic stem cell lines safer for patients than Thomson's original cell lines?

2. What good does Thomson see in the Bush administration's 2001 compromise allowing federal funding of embryonic stem cell research only for existing cell lines?

3. In the author's view, how could *studying* embryonic stem cells actually make researchers *less* dependent on embryonic stem cells?

A *lan Boyle: In terms of stem cell technology, there was an advance in getting beyond the mouse feeder cells [that contaminated early stem cell lines], but there are still some animal components that need to be used to support human embryonic stem cells. Do you think that problem is solvable?*

James Thomson: I think there are going to be a couple of things that will ultimately change federal policy, though we might have to wait for [the end of the Bush administration]. One is that my group and quite a few other groups are developing culture conditions that are much better than the original culture conditions. . . . My prediction is [that by 2007] there will be at least one and probably several publications demonstrating that: completely defined conditions, no animal products, no feeder layers of either human or animal origins.

The other thing, which is already happening, is that more and more clinically relevant lineages are being published. People have published work with dopaminergic neurons, motor neurons, heart cells—quite a list now. That means that although we're not ready to put these cells into patients yet, the clock is ticking.

Patient Safety Demands
New Stem Cell Lines

And the original cell lines, while they can be put into patients if you jump through enough hoops, they're clearly not the safest things there, because no matter how much testing you do, you might have missed something. If you derive stem cells from day one in completely defined conditions, in the appropriate GLP [Good Laboratory Practice] conditions, there's simply going to be a higher level of safety. So if I were a patient—say, 10 years down the line when the therapies come on board—which cell line would I want? I wouldn't want the original ones.

When we derived those original cell lines, I was very consciously making them just for experimental purposes, because I figured other people would derive them under these GLP conditions and I wouldn't have to deal with that. We'd just do the experiments. Little did I know that we'd be stuck with these cell lines [because President Bush limited federal funding to preexisting cell lines in 2001].

It hasn't bothered me yet, because we didn't really know how to make them better. But the field is changing now. We're getting very close to where we can make them under completely defined conditions. And as I said, I suspect there will be multiple people publishing on that. So I hope that that will drive the political process. . . .

Bush Support for Limited Research Was Better than No Support

In the first four years, it was entirely about the basic science. Although a lot of the scientists have been very vocal about the compromise [announced in August 2001], I've been kind of quiet about it. And the reason is that, in a kind of "silver lining to the dark cloud" thing, it's almost better that Bush was elected. I don't know how to say this without offending someone, but it's a little bit like Nixon going to China. Nixon didn't suddenly become a Communist.

President Clinton did not fund this research. It's nice to yell at the Republicans, but moderate Republicans have been some of the biggest supporters of this. Even though it's a

Existing Embryonic Stem Cell Lines Are Contaminated

Currently available lines of human embryonic stem cells have been contaminated with a non-human molecule that compromises their potential therapeutic use in human subjects, according to research by investigators at the University of California, San Diego (UCSD) School of Medicine and the Salk Institute in La Jolla, California.

In a study published online January 23, 2005, in the journal *Nature Medicine*, the researchers found that human embryonic stem cells, including those currently approved for study under federal funding in the U.S., contain a non-human, cell-surface sialic acid called N-glycolylneuraminic acid (Neu5Gc), even though human cells are genetically unable to make it. . . .

In studies with one of the federally approved human embryonic stem cell lines, the investigators determined that the Neu5Gc is incorporated by the stem cells when they are grown or derived from laboratory cultures that contain animal sources of the non-human Neu5Gc molecule. All traditional culture-dish methods used to grow all human embryonic stem cells include animal-derived materials, including connective tissue cells (so-called "feeder layers") from mice and fetal calf serum.

Sue Pondrom, "Current Human Embryonic Stem Cell Lines Contaminated," University of California, San Diego, public release, January 23, 2005.

compromise, and even though the compromise does not represent good public policy, it got the field going, it got federal funding going for the first time. Scientists suddenly knew that if there was a change in administration, it wouldn't stop—whereas if Bush didn't allow it to go forward, the policy could flip-flop every time a Democrat or a Republican takes the White House. So even though we have to go beyond that policy, it did get the field started, and I think that's a positive way of looking at it.

During that first four years, [using only existing stem cell lines] probably didn't hurt things that much—it did create this funny bottleneck about cell lines, which did slow things down, and that's unfortunate. But going forward another three years, it could actually hurt people. Just because it's going to take us 10 years to derive these new therapies doesn't mean we don't want to have the cell lines now.

It's a long-term process to really characterize these lines well. The existing cell lines have been around for seven years, and people are gearing up to want to do clinical trials. They've been arguing with the FDA [Food and Drug Administration] all this time over the original cell lines. Well, that means we want the new cell lines now for some therapy that's going to be 10 years out.

A three-year difference could really hurt people now, because the [culture] media has gotten qualitatively different. Just deriving the same old cell lines with the same problems made no sense to me, but once those conditions are really defined and safe, then it makes sense to go back and derive more. So I hope public policy allows that.

Current public policy in theory allows it, because you are allowed to use private funding, but the reality is that the federal government, the National Institutes of Health, is the funding that drives basic research and research into new therapies in this country. And if you exclude that, then you're basically stuck....

Non-Embryonic Cells Are No Substitute

How do you respond to the claim that we have these other sources of stem cells—adult stem cells or cord blood—and there's no need to turn to embryonic cells?

We don't. The most studied cell in the whole body, in terms of stem cells, is the hematopoietic [blood-forming] stem cell. It can't be grown. So what you do when you do a bone marrow transplant is you take some bone marrow out of you—actually, we do peripheral blood—and we put [it] in another patient without expanding it. There's a clinical need for that expansion step, but it can't be done right now. And hundreds of labs for 30 years have studied that adult stem cell, and that's the one we know the most about.

If you go to these other ones, most of them are known by indirect methods, and nobody can actually isolate and expand and grow them in useful ways. But we can already make blood in very reasonable quantities from human embryonic cells. . . .

So if you think about particular things, you can find a stem cell that might work for that application, but this ability to expand these cells in an unlimited, stable developmental state is essentially unprecedented among stem cells. . . . People can do mesenchymal stem cells [from bone marrow] pretty well, and neural stem cells kind of well, but neural stem cells is a good example. If you try to make dopaminergic neurons from fetal neural stem cells, you get a burst of that activity, and it goes away. Nobody's been able to sustainably make dopaminergic neurons from an adult stem cell, or a fetal one, period—whereas with embryonic cells you can do it already. Over time that might change. But a lot of good groups have tried very hard and failed, to date.

And again, getting back to the basic science thing: If we study the embryonic stem cells, we learn the basic science. That knowledge is just as likely to be applied to adult stem cells as to the embryonic stem cells. The knowledge goes back and forth. And in the case of the blood, people have failed at growing that cell for three decades. Well, studying that lineage with embryonic stem cells, we might learn the clues to make it growable, and it might be that we still want to use adult stem cells to do that because there are a lot of advantages to that, but the knowledge might come from embryonic stem cells.

This divide about adult vs. embryonic, it's a political debate, it's not a scientific debate. Scientists choose the model for a question that fits the question.... So people who have focused on adult stem cells historically are using embryonic stem cells now. It doesn't mean that's what they think will be the therapy, but they see it as a more useful model to understand the questions they want to ask.

> *"Recent biological advances have raised encouraging possibilities for producing powerful stem cells without harming embryos."*

Using Alternative Sources of Stem Cells Resolves Ethical Issues

Domestic Policy Council

In the following viewpoint, the White House's Domestic Policy Council advocates five approaches to stem cell research as ethical alternatives to the destruction of human embryos: cell extraction from already dead embryos; non-harmful biopsy of living embryos; cell extraction from nonembryonic cellular systems; reprogramming of adult cells back to an undifferentiated (pluripotent) state; and cell extraction from amniotic fluid. The Domestic Policy Council, directed by Karl Zinsmeister, coordinates the domestic policy-making process for the U.S. president, monitors the implementation of President George W. Bush's domestic policies, and represents the president's priorities to other branches of government.

Domestic Policy Council, "Advancing Stem Cell Science Without Destroying Human Life," The White House, April 2, 2007, www.whitehouse.gov.

As you read, consider the following questions:

1. What most valuable quality of embryonic stem cells do scientists aim to produce in alternative sources, as described by the Domestic Policy Council?

2. According to the authors, how have researchers from the Harvard Stem Cell Institute and Japan's Institute for Frontier Medical Science reprogrammed ordinary adult cells into a pluripotent state?

3. What uses of amniotic stem cells have already been demonstrated by Wake Forest University researchers, according to the Domestic Policy Council?

The destruction of embryos for experimental purposes could open the way to more general and profound manipulations and reengineerings of human life. Without an understanding that life begins at conception, and that an embryo is a nascent human being, there will always be arguments that other uses, takeovers, and makeovers of embryos are justified by potential scientific and medical benefits. Crossing this line would needlessly encourage a conflict between science and ethics that can only do damage to both, and to our nation as a whole....

A policy that defends the inviolability of human life does not preclude the hopeful possibilities of new findings and new therapies. It simply means we must harness the creative powers of our advancing knowledge only to humane and morally balanced means and ends. Amidst today's dizzying pace of technological innovation, it is worth taking care to make sure that our moral and ethical policies keep up. The biotechnology revolution will bring sound and wholesome human results over the long run only if it is sensibly governed.

The stem cell debate is only the first in what will be an onrushing train of biotechnology challenges in our future. We must establish a constructive precedent here for taking the moral dimensions of these issues seriously. We must make certain we don't force ourselves into a false choice between science and ethics—because we need *both*.

And there is good reason, and growing scientific evidence, to believe that we can have both. . . .

Advances in Alternative Sources of Pluripotent Cells

Recent biological advances have raised encouraging possibilities for producing powerful stem cells without harming human embryos. What scientists value most about embryonic stem cells is their pluripotency and expandability—that they have the potential to be teased into many, and perhaps all, of the different cell types in the body. But scientists have begun to find that this potential may also exist in certain cells derived without embryos. New ways of producing pluripotent cells that don't require the destruction (or even endangerment) of human embryos are now being investigated.

In May 2005, the President's Council on Bioethics published *Alternative Sources of Human Pluripotent Stem Cells*, a White Paper which suggested four possible approaches for alternative sources: (1) by extracting viable cells from embryos already dead; (2) by non-harmful biopsy of living embryos; (3) by extracting cells from artificially created non-embryonic cellular systems or entities (engineered to lack the essential elements of an embryo); (4) by reprogramming (or dedifferentiation) of adult cells back to pluripotency. Each of these methods carries its own scientific and ethical uncertainties, but one or more may ultimately offer a path toward an ethically responsible source of pluripotent stem cells.

In January 2007, landmark research from Wake Forest University has suggested yet another alternative: Amniotic

Extracting Stem Cells from Amniotic Fluid Does Not Harm Embryos

Researchers at Wake Forest University and Harvard University reported [in January 2007] that the stem cells they drew from amniotic fluid donated by pregnant women hold much the same promise as embryonic stem cells.

They reported they were able to extract the stem cells from the fluid, which cushions babies in the womb, without harm to mother or fetus and turn their discovery into several different tissue cell types, including brain, liver and bone. . . .

One of the more promising aspects of the research is that some of the DNA of the amnio stem cells contained Y chromosomes, which means the cells came from the babies rather than the pregnant moms.

Associated Press, "Stem Cells Found in Amniotic Fluid,"
MSNBC.com, January 8, 2007.

fluid, investigators discovered, contains highly flexible stem cells shed by the fetus. These appear to have all the valuable qualities of embryonic stem cells, plus some advantages of their own—like greater ease and speed of culture, and no tendency to produce tumors. Meanwhile, they are comparatively easy to collect without harming human life. . . .

The Promise of Somatic Cell Reprogramming

Just in the short period since they were sketched out in May 2005, significant progress has been made on [the four techniques identified by the Bioethics Council], as reported in a number of new, peer-reviewed research studies published in leading scientific journals. At this point, one of the most promising avenues appears to be somatic cell reprogramming, which uses chemical and genetic factors to reprogram an adult cell to function like an embryonic stem cell.

Each cell in an individual's body has the same DNA as every other cell. But in the course of developing into specialized adult tissues, different cells undergo different patterns of gene activation. Somatic cell reprogramming seeks to switch on or off the appropriate genes to transform an adult cell back into the equivalent of an embryonic stem cell. This might be accomplished by stimulating the adult cell with the right combination of chemicals and genes, or by exposing it to the cytoplasm of an existing line of stem cells. This method could, in theory, create stem cells in bulk while bypassing entirely the problem of creating and destroying embryos.

Two research teams that have demonstrated significant progress toward this sort of cell reprogramming are Kevin Eggan and Chad Cowan from the Harvard Stem Cell Institute, and Shinya Yamanaka and Kazutoshi Takahashi from the Department of Stem Cell Biology at Japan's Institute for Frontier Medical Science. In August of 2005 and August of 2006, respectively, each team published impressive results which seemed to produce pluripotent stem cells by reprogramming ordinary adult cells.

The project conducted at the Harvard Stem Cell Institute fused a human adult cell with an embryonic stem cell. (These could come from one of the embryonic stem cell lines that President George W. Bush has approved for use with federal funds.) That effectively turned back the clock on the adult cell such that it was reprogrammed to a pluripotent state. Eggan and Cowan believe that their research could lead to "an alternative route for creating genetically tailored human embryonic stem cells for use in the study and treatment of disease."

Drs. Yamanaka and Takahashi published research based on mouse cells. Their complex study produced stunningly simple results: They reprogrammed adult cells into a pluripotent state simply by bathing them in four genetic factors. "The finding is an important step in controlling pluripotency, which may eventually allow the creation of pluripotent cells directly from somatic cells of patients," comments Dr. Yamanaka. If successful, this could offer all the benefits of embryonic stem cells and more—these cells could be genetically matched to any prospective patient—without the ethical dilemmas of embryonic destruction.

Extracting Stem Cells from Amniotic Fluid

Other promising avenues are likely to open in the future. The latest alternative, published on January 7, 2007, in *Nature Biotechnology*, involves amniotic-fluid stem cells. Dr. Anthony Atala and a team from the Institute for Regenerative Medicine at Wake Forest University School of Medicine and the Harvard Medical School reported on a new category of readily available stem cells extractable from the waters cushioning babies in utero, as well as the placenta. While this very new research will need to be replicated and confirmed, Dr. Atala and colleagues have already managed to grow useful brain, bone, liver, muscle, and other replacement tissues using these stem cells.

This discovery suggests that if all U.S. newborns had their amniotic stem cells frozen, they could be available for future tissue replacement without fear of immune rejection. Moreover, a bank of amniotic stem cells from the waters of 100,000 pregnancies could supply 99 percent of the U.S. population with genetically compatible stem cells for possible transplantation. More studies will be needed to confirm that amniotic stem cells can generate all other cell types, but so far every culture attempted has succeeded. It must also be determined that tests conducted in mice will translate to humans.

"Too many unanswered questions remain about these proposals to [determine] whether any of them are ethical methods for obtaining embryonic stem cells."

Using Alternative Sources of Stem Cells Does Not Resolve Ethical Issues

Daniel McConchie

In the following viewpoint, Daniel McConchie considers four imaginative proposals for obtaining embryonic stem cells without destroying human embryos, and concludes that all of them still raise serious ethical concerns. Some potentially harm a human embryo; others create cellular entities that could be viewed as equivalent to an embryo, which, McConchie argues, deserve the same protections and status as living human embryos and must not be destroyed for research. Daniel McConchie holds a master's degree in Christian thought with an emphasis in bioethics from Trinity Evangelical Divinity School in Deerfield, Illinois. He is vice president and chief of staff of Americans United for Life, an anti-abortion organization based in Chicago.

As you read, consider the following questions:

1. Why are the parthenote method and the alternate nuclear transfer method ethically objectionable, according to McConchie?

2. What two ethical issues make the morula proposal unlikely to succeed as an alternative to the destruction of embryos, in the author's opinion?

3. If it is ethically acceptable to remove organs for transplant from a brain-dead person, why does McConchie object to removing stem cells from a "brain-dead" embryo?

In an attempt to cool the [stem cell] debate, some researchers have offered imaginative new ways to obtain embryonic stem cells without the necessary step of destroying living human embryos. . . .

The Parthenote Proposal

One of the earliest of these new proposals is the idea to create a parthenote—an egg that develops into an embryo and creates embryonic stem cells. New research has shown that a chemical trigger can cause an egg to begin dividing and organizing—even eggs that have failed to be fertilized by a sperm. Reproductive clinics throw away thousands of eggs that have failed to be fertilized through multiple in vitro fertilization (IVF) attempts. Because mammalian parthenotes cannot develop very far due to the lack of paternal DNA, many researchers do not consider them embryos but "embryo-like" entities.

Method: Since eggs have only half of the requisite DNA, they would have to be obtained from women before the final maturation process (before ovulation) when the egg still has a full DNA complement, or the eggs would have to copy their own 23 chromosomes to produce 46 chromosomes when exposed to a chemical trigger. Such a trigger or an electrical shock tricks the egg into believing that it has been fertilized. Upon reaching the blastocyst stage, the parthenote would be broken apart and its stem cells harvested.

Technical Challenges: Because of the faulty genetic structure of parthenotes, there are questions about whether stem cells derived from them could be used for treatments. The impact of seriously genetically flawed stem cells is unknown. Incidents of cancer could be higher than the 25% typical when using other embryonic cells. In addition, the available pool of genotypes for research would be limited since only fertile females can be used.

Ethical Issues: The largest ethical issue is the question over whether a parthenote is an embryo, and there is little consensus. Some argue that it is not an embryo because it can never develop, while others hold that it should be treated like an embryo unless it can be proven otherwise.

The Morula Proposal

Reproductive Genetics Institute (RGI) in Chicago is one of the world's leading experts in pre-implantation genetic diagnosis (PGD)—a procedure where a cell is removed from a developing embryo and analyzed. Some use this procedure to identify whether a developing embryo has a genetic disorder such as Tay-Saks or Huntington's disease. Only those embryos passing the genetic test are implanted. The others are destroyed.

Scientists at RGI are claiming a new distinction—a way around the current objection to pursuing human embryonic stem cell research. Instead of destroying living human embryos, RGI scientists think they can use the same principles of obtaining cells for PGD to develop embryonic stem cell lines.

Method: Scientists would take an early-embryo that has developed to about the 8-cell stage (called a morula), and remove a single cell. They would then attempt to coax that cell to replicate into an embryonic stem cell line. The embryo (less the one cell) could then be transferred to a womb.

The Use of "Dedifferentiated" Cells Could Still Be Viewed as Unethical

Could people be the source of their own cell lines by somehow inducing their cells to return to the embryonic state, in which each cell was capable of becoming any type of cell? Embryologists call the process by which embryonic cells transform themselves into the various tissues of the human body "differentiation." Returning cells to their edenic plasticity is known, therefore, as "dedifferentiation." If—a very big "if"—this could be routinely accomplished, the problem of finding immunologically compatible cells to put into people's bodies would disappear because their own cells would be the template.

But would what's been unfortunately dubbed "the holy grail" of stem cells, dedifferentiation, satisfy the moral critics? Five years ago, I thought it probably would. Today I am less confident. The same moral logic that resists creating lines with cells carved from healthy early embryos might also see a fully dedifferentiated cell, able to become any kind of human tissue, as a sort of embryo, albeit one in need of special care if it is to develop into a healthy baby.

Thomas H. Murray, "Will New Ways of Creating Stem Cells Dodge the Objections?" Hastings Center Report, January–February 2005.

Technical Challenges: The largest technical challenge to this proposal is getting a single stem cell to replicate sufficiently to turn into stem cell line. Currently, scientists wait until the blastocyst stage where the embryo has developed into several hundred cells, break the embryo apart to obtain the cells, and use all the available cells to create a line. Even with hundreds of cells, scientists have a difficult time creating cell lines. Doing so requires dozens if not hundreds of embryos. Robert Lanza at Advanced Cell Technology (ACT) in Massachusetts has said that he believes this single cell process can produce stem cell lines, but procedures do not yet exist.

Ethical Issues: There are two primary ethical issues with this proposal. First, it requires a method that is potentially harmful to the embryo. While hundreds of children have been born using PGD, we do not yet know the consequence of taking a cell from the very early embryo. Second, at the morula stage, twinning is still possible; that is to say, it is possible that the obtained cell could be an embryo itself—the single cell may be able to develop if implanted into a womb.

The Organ Transplant Proposal

Fifty years after the first successful organ transplant, Donald Landry and Howard Zucker of Columbia University in New York think that the same principles used today to harvest organs from those at the edge of death can be used to find a way out of the current embryonic stem cell morass.

Modern organ transplant rules follow the following general principle: a person's body does not have to be totally dead for it to be "dead enough" to ethically remove vital tissues for transplant. Because the line between life and death is not precise, this principle has been accepted and is used to allow a definition of death other than complete death of every cell in the body. This allows the transplantation of living tissue from an otherwise "dead" person.

In this proposal, scientists argue that embryos exist that are, in essence, dead just like those who are brain dead with functioning organs. The term "arrested development" is often used to denote embryos that are believed will never develop further. Landry and Zucker estimate that 60% of human embryos in cryopreservation are in a state of "arrested development."

Method: Scientists hope to identify arrested development embryos whose stem cells are functional, obtain the stem cells (using the standard method of breaking embryos apart), and develop stem cell lines for research and possible future treatment.

Technical Challenges: No test currently exists to determine whether an embryo that is not developing is truly dead. Landry and Zucker are working to develop tools to measure the chemical and genetic signatures of embryos after 24 hours of non-development.

There is a question about whether the embryonic stem cells obtained from such embryos would be useful. It is possible that failure to create stem cell lines from "surplus" IVF embryos is due to the failure of the cell from "dead" embryos to replicate.

Ethical Issues: Is it possible to identify a "brain death" criterion for embryos? This is uncertain. There simply is no test similar to that which determines brain death. Chemical and genetic signatures would measure seemingly arbitrary criterion, particularly since we know so little about embryology (and especially compared to current understandings of a fully-developed nervous system that governs the brain death criterion).

The Alternate Nuclear Transfer (ANT) Proposal

Suggested by Stanford physician and ethicist William Hurlbut, alternate nuclear transfer (ANT) is similar to cloning. Using the cloning method, scientists would create an embryo or "embryo-like entity" that lacks a developmental gene. The entity would be similar to those that generally develop into a cancerous tumor—an entity that most scientists and ethicists consider never to have been an embryo.

Method: A developmental gene is turned off in the nucleus about to be transferred. Using the normal cloning process, the changed nucleus is then inserted into an enucleated egg, stimulated to divide, and stem cells are harvested when the resulting embryo or entity reaches the blastocyst stage.

Technical Challenges: Currently, the proposed method would be both difficult and expensive; the difficulties of cloning are compounded by the difficulties of genetic alteration. It likely would be a number of years before this method was successful, and, due to the technical hurdles of genetic manipulation, cloning technology, and stem cell cultivation, even longer before [the method became] reasonable.

Ethical Issues: The core question for most ethicists is whether the entity created is a non-embryo or a disabled embryo. Hurlbut suggests that because the entity lacks a developmental/organizational gene and could never develop, it is never an embryo, thus no embryo is destroyed. Others, such as Richard Doerflinger of the U.S. Conference of Catholic Bishops, argue that if the knocked out gene offers several days of development, the entity is an embryo for that period of time, and only later ceases to be such.

The answer to the question of whether an embryo-like entity that cannot develop is an embryo or not is likely the same for both parthenotes and ANT.

Too Many Ethical Questions Remain

Currently, Christians oppose embryonic stem cell research for several interconnected reasons. Most importantly, it requires the destruction of human embryos. But also, using embryonic stem cells on human beings likely constitutes a violation of proper ethical considerations regarding experimentation on human subjects. This is in part due to the lack of proper animal modeling and experimentation. This is particularly important in light of current alternative methods of disease treatment for many of the ailments considered possible targets for future embryonic stem cell therapies.

Currently, too many unanswered questions remain about these proposals to be able to move ahead with determining whether any of them are ethical methods for obtaining embryonic stem cells. We must take the cautious route by not pursuing them in human research until it is clear from animal studies that the entity in question is in fact not an embryo.

The Morula Proposal is unique in that it does not require breaking apart an entity that might or might not be an embryo; the question is whether the early embryonic cell is itself totipotent—capable of further developing in the same way that you and I developed from a single cell. Even if we assume that this is not the case, given the possibility of possible unknown danger for the developing embryo (no treatment option currently provides an overriding ethical justification for exposing an embryo to such unknown risk), this method still cannot be justified at this time.

As a final note, all other objections aside, we do not yet have sufficient knowledge from animal models to justify the pursuit of any embryonic stem cell research in humans. While pursuing in animal studies the knowledgebase that might justify human trials, these methods of obtaining such cells should be used so that we might have as much knowledge as possible for determining potential ethical means of obtaining embryonic stem cells if or when it becomes necessary to do so.

"We urge national authorities to establish a . . . system of national oversight
for stem cell transplantation studies."

Ethical Stem Cell Research Requires Federal Funding and Oversight

Jonathan Kimmelman, Françoise Baylis, and Kathleen Cranley Glass

Stem cell research has already taken some ethical missteps that could be corrected and avoided with more federal oversight and less restriction of federal funding, Jonathan Kimmelman, Françoise Baylis, and Kathleen Cranley Glass contend in the following viewpoint. The authors argue that federal review of research studies, a central registry of all current research, and nationally established research guidelines would minimize scientific fraud, financial conflicts of interest, and unrealistic claims about the potential benefits of stem cell technology. Jonathan Kimmelman researches ethical and social problems of biotechnology in the Biomedical Ethics Unit of McGill University in Montreal.

Jonathan Kimmelman, Françoise Baylis, and Kathleen Cranley Glass, "Stem Cell Trials: Lessons from Gene Transfer Research," *Hastings Center Report*, vol. 36, no. 1, January–February 2006, pp. 23–26. Copyright © 2006 Hastings Center. Reproduced by permission.

Françoise Baylis is professor of bioethics and philosophy at Dalhousie University in Halifax, Nova Scotia. Kathleen Cranley Glass is an associate professor of human genetics and director of the Biomedical Ethics Unit at McGill.

As you read, consider the following questions:

1. What evidence do the authors offer that stem cell technology has been "oversold"?
2. How does restriction of federal funding for stem cell research make ethically risky financial conflicts of interest more likely, according to the authors?
3. Why is the need for federal oversight even greater for stem cell research than for gene transfer research, another cutting-edge technology that raises ethical issues?

Since 1998, when James Thomson and John Gearhart reported the first successful derivation of human embryonic stem cells and human embryonic germ cells, respectively, the scientific community has championed the therapeutic potential of these cells. Indeed, despite the restrictions on embryo research in some jurisdictions and despite the 2006 controversy surrounding the validity of the stem cell research conducted by Woo Suk Hwang, stem cells may soon enter their first human trials—possibly within a year.

Stem cell transplantation will not be the first biotechnology to begin trials amid revolutionary expectations and moral apprehension. More than fifteen years ago, the first experiments with gene transfer in human somatic cells inspired similar hopes and fears. Gene transfer quickly evolved into a competitive research area, but its progress was checked by ethical missteps. With embryonic stem cells poised to begin human trials, now is an opportune time for scientists and ethicists to review some of gene transfer's ethical miscues.

Moving Too Quickly

From the first protocol involving humans, gene transfer was caught up in ethical controversy. In 1980, hematologist Martin Cline began gene transfer trials without prior approval from his institutional review board (IRB); neither the National Institutes of Health (which supported the study) nor committees at a collaborating institution in Israel were apprised of the fact that his protocols involved recombinant DNA. The studies were faulted for their scientific prematurity, and Cline became the first clinical investigator to be formally sanctioned by the NIH for violating human subjects regulations. In 1992, another controversy erupted when the NIH recommended canceling a contract of a prominent gene transfer researcher, Steven Rosenberg, for pursuing trials without sufficient preclinical data. Episodes like these created early impressions that gene transfer researchers were moving into human studies too aggressively.

There are various indications that some prominent stem cell researchers have not fully absorbed gene transfer's cautionary lessons. . . . Cloning pioneer Woo Suk Hwang has admitted to ethical improprieties in obtaining human eggs and is under investigation for scientific fraud. Elsewhere, two different research groups (one backed by Geron, the other by ES Cell International) are reportedly nearing human studies despite concerns expressed by many about the safety and prematurity of such trials. . . .

Overselling the Science

Over the years, some gene transfer enthusiasts have advanced extravagant claims about its promise. Yet despite almost seven hundred approved trials in the United States, no gene therapies have been approved for clinical use in the United States or Europe. Only a few trials are regarded as showing efficacy, and important questions remain regarding the safety of these interventions.

Americans Support Federal Regulation of Stem Cell Research

Surveys show a majority of Americans support strong federal oversight of stem-cell research and other new human genetic technologies.... Without effective regulation, however, [these technologies] could also lead to greater health inequities, harm to women who provide eggs for research, and misguided efforts to produce cloned or genetically modified children. It is imperative that our political leaders begin formulating bipartisan proposals for regulatory structures that will allow us to reap the benefits and avoid the risks that these technologies hold.

Richard Hayes,
"Does the Senate Vote on Stem-Cell Research Matter?"
San Francisco Chronicle, *July 19, 2006, p. B-9.*

The 1995 NIH panel that criticized gene therapy studies for not yielding useful information also admonished gene transfer investigators for creating a "widely held, but mistaken, perception that clinical gene therapy is already highly successful." Unrealistic portrayals of medical potential cloud ethical deliberations by promoting the therapeutic misconception, undermining the scientific aspects of trials, and drawing attention away from the risks that such experiments pose to research participants. When elevated expectations collide with scientific setbacks or publicized mishaps, a field's credibility suffers.

Stem cell transplantation research shows some indications of following a similar course—witness slogans like "save lives with stem cells," used to promote California's Proposition 71. Like gene transfer research, which adopted the term "gene *therapy*" long before safety and efficacy had been established, stem cell research has embraced terms such as "*therapeutic* cloning" that threaten to obfuscate the ethical issues. A second important parallel has been the attempt to defuse controversy by reconstructing terminology. Just as "human genetic engineering" was replaced by "gene therapy," "cloning" may give way to the less charged "nuclear transplantation"—as a group of scientists argued in a 2002 essay, "Please Don't Call It Cloning," in *Science*.

News reports also commonly contain overreaching assertions. In many instances, cell researchers have attempted to caution the public against unrealistic expectations, but not always. After Ron Reagan, in his address to the Democratic National Convention, implied that a stem cell cure for Parkinson's disease could be widely available in ten years, leading researchers like John Gearhart went on record praising Reagan for doing "a good job."

Lastly, excitement about a new intervention's therapeutic possibilities can easily obscure unresolved safety questions. Safety concerns about ex vivo gene transfer have been reawakened following the unexpected development of leukemia in three volunteers (one of whom died) in an apparently successful study on the use of gene transfer to treat a type of severe combined immunodeficiency. These concerns parallel the uncertainties surrounding the tumorigenic [tumor-causing] potential of transplanted, stem cell-derived tissues. . . .

Conflicts of Interest and Full Disclosure

Financial conflicts of interest for individuals and institutions are likely to loom large in stem cell transplantation trials. Partly this is because restrictions in U.S. federal funding of stem cell research have driven much of the research into the private sector. Companies such as Geron, which holds exclusive rights to therapies and diagnostics derived from some of the first stem cell lines, may exert a significant influence over the development and availability of stem cell technologies. Additionally, in the period since the earliest gene transfer trials, the relationship between academia and the private sector has been reconfigured; university researchers are encouraged even more strongly today to patent their work, to court venture capitalists, and to develop spinoff companies. These developments are likely to amplify challenges in assuring ethical rigor in stem cell transplantation studies.

There is a particular need for researchers in new fields to be forthcoming with information that can improve the safety of trials and enable the public to remain informed about the field's progress. Gene transfer investigators, while held by the NIH to unusually high standards of public disclosure, have not always shared safety information willingly. [For example], an investigation by the NIH revealed that over six hundred adverse events involving adenovirus-based vectors had not been reported to the NIH as required under its guidelines.

The environment for stem cell transplantation research may again prove to be public disclosure's antagonist. A public/private divide in the rules governing research in the United States and the overwhelmingly private sponsorship of stem cell research could shelter many investigators from obligatory public reporting. The politically sensitive nature of stem cell research may also discourage investigators from volunteering trial information to the public. Nevertheless, transparency advances several ethical ends. Trials have little scientific value unless their results are disseminated, and pooling adverse event information allows immature fields to quickly identify safety concerns. In addition, the public cannot meaningfully participate in stem cell transplantation policy discussions unless it receives current information on the progress of research.

Three Recommendations

1. A National Body Should Oversee Stem Cell Transplantation Studies. Gene transfer research has benefited from the existence in several countries of national bodies that publicly re-

view protocols and address questions of safety, quality, and ethics. We urge national authorities to establish a similar system of national oversight for stem cell transplantation studies. This recommendation is consistent with research guidelines and relevant legislation in Canada and the United Kingdom, but contrary to a recent report from the U.S. National Academy of Sciences, which recommends a system of national oversight but does not recommend centralized review of research protocols.

Unfortunately, the federal ban on funding research involving the derivation of stem cells restricts the U.S. government's ability to require centralized review of stem cell transplantation studies. Alternatives to federal oversight should therefore be contemplated. One possibility would be the creation of an interstate review committee by states funding stem cell research; such a body would emulate the original Recombinant DNA Advisory Committee's system for reviewing gene transfer protocols. Short of such concerted state efforts, professional societies with an interest in stem cells might devise a system for the voluntary review and public reporting of transplantation protocols.

2. A Mandatory International Registry of Studies Should Be Established. We recommend another salutary practice well established for gene transfer: the establishment of an international registry of human studies. . . . Trial registration would provide a means for scientists, policy-makers, ethicists, and the public to remain abreast of ongoing work on stem cell transplantation.

3. A National Panel Should Be Created to Set Guidelines for Studies. Stem cell transplantation studies raise ethical and scientific questions not routinely encountered in clinical research. For example, transplantation investigators may need to devise consent language to convey "moral" risk related to stem cell derivation. Stem cell researchers might also develop a set of standards and guidelines intended to maximize the value of

information sought in human studies. Given the politically sensitive nature of stem cell tissues, transplantation researchers might also wish to discourage members of their field from pursuing studies aimed at medical enhancements.

Although the NAS guidelines for the responsible practice of stem cell research offer very little comment on transplantation trial ethics, they do call for the establishment of a national body to "assess periodically the adequacy of the guidelines proposed ... and to provide a forum for a continuing discussion of issues involved in [stem] cell research." The mandate of this body could usefully be expanded to explicitly refer to stem cell transplantation research. Consistent with the NAS recommendation, we recommend that a high-level national panel of scientists and ethicists be convened to devise national ethical guidelines for stem cell transplantation studies.

The need for such measures may be heightened by one way stem cell research is significantly different from gene transfer research. Whereas the latter is now regarded as a natural extension of practices like bone marrow transplantation, stem cell research raises some special ethical and political issues, including the moral status of embryos, informed consent from egg/embryo donors, and the acceptability of treating embryonic tissues as mere commodities. The politicization of debates over these issues may cause some investigators to bristle at what they consider to be ethical roadblocks to transplantation research, but the penalties for failing to appreciate the complex ethical terrain are likely to be greater than has been the case for gene transfer research.

| "Where federal funding is most lavish and regulation is most onerous, that is where progress in getting treatments to patients is slowing down."

Ethical Stem Cell Research Does Not Depend on Federal Funding or Oversight

Ronald Bailey

In the following viewpoint, science and technology writer Ronald Bailey argues that President George W. Bush's restriction of federal funding for embryonic stem cell research in 2001 actually galvanized scientific advance: A flood of state and private funding followed, researchers broadened their hunt for alternative sources of stem cells, and competition to fund the most promising (and potentially most profitable) work increased. Ronald Bailey is the science correspondent for the libertarian magazine Reason *and the author of* Liberation Biology: The Moral and Scientific Case for the Biotech Revolution.

Ronald Bailey, "The Rise of Stem Cell Research: Did George Bush Inadvertently Jump-start a Stem Cell Revolution?" *ReasonOnline*, January 19, 2007, www.reason.com. Copyright © 2007 by Reason Foundation, 3415 S. Sepulveda Blvd., Suite 400, Los Angeles, CA 90034, www.reason.com. Reproduced by permission.

As you read, consider the following questions:

1. According to the author, how much money has been allocated for embryonic stem cell research in California alone since federal funding was cut?

2. How does the development of assisted reproductive techniques (ART) suggest that stem cell research can be far more successful without federal oversight than with it, according to Bailey?

3. How does Bailey dispute the truism among researchers and economists that federal funding is necessary for basic research?

Democrats in the House of Representatives passed legislation [in January 2007] that would lift President [George W.] Bush's restrictions on federal funding of embryonic stem cell research. Bush issued his only veto against the same legislation in 2006. The legislation would allow federal funding for developing new embryonic stem cell lines derived from donated embryos leftover from fertility treatments.

When Bush first restricted federal funding to embryonic stem lines derived before his nationally televised speech on the subject in 2001, researchers feared that such limits would send a signal that would strongly "chill" research in the field. For example, many researchers worried that Sen. Sam Brownback's (R-Kan.) bill to ban both publicly and privately financed therapeutic cloning research was just the first step toward outlawing all human embryonic stem cell research. But that didn't happen.

Federal Spending Cuts Sparked Massive State and Private Funding

Instead, the research restrictions—real and proposed—provoked a strong pushback by researchers and eventually the public. States began big time funding of embryonic stem cell research, e.g., $3 billion in California and $270 million in New

Harvard's Research Program Follows Ethical Guidelines

Harvard University announced [in June 2006] the launch of a privately funded, multimillion-dollar program to create cloned human embryos as sources of medically promising stem cells. . . .

Harvard officials said they had developed their program over a two-year period under an umbrella of new ethics rules, and hoped to boost the field without unduly offending opponents. . . .

Much of the ethical wrangling leading up to [the] announcement related to the procurement of human eggs. Under rules ultimately approved by all eight ethics review boards with jurisdiction over the experiments, women will be reimbursed for expenses they directly incur in the process of donating eggs but will not be eligible for the thousands of dollars they could get for providing eggs to a fertility clinic to help other women get pregnant.

Rick Weiss, "Harvard Announces Private Project to Make Human Stem Cells," Washington Post, June 7, 2006, p. A10. Copyright © 2006 The Washington Post. Reprinted with permission.

Jersey. And the floodgates of private funding opened, showering hundreds of millions on stem cell researchers. It is highly probable that far more embryos have been used for stem cell research than would have been the case had President Bush not imposed his restrictions. How's that for irony!

Although we'll never know for sure, it is also probable that the fear that further limits might be imposed on human embryonic stem cell research intensified the hunt for other sources of stem cells. And the very good news is that these searches have been very successful. Stem cells have been found in fat, testicles, umbilical cord blood and tissue, bone marrow, and, most recently, amniotic fluid. More therapies using adult stem cells should be soon available in the medical marketplace. In fact, stem cell research may be enhanced as states compete to fund the most promising work. Maybe.

Research Stalls When the Feds Get Involved

Instead of being modeled on drug development, perhaps embryonic stem cell research will follow a development path more like that blazed by researchers in assisted reproduction. Rather than being hampered by a paucity of federal research funding perhaps embryonic stem cell research will flourish just as research on assisted reproduction techniques (ART) has. Arguably in vitro fertilization research has proceeded rapidly because of, not in spite of, essentially no federal funding. So far more than 3 million babies have been born by means of ART. Without intrusive federal oversight and regulation IVF researchers have been able to deploy new techniques such as intracytoplasmic sperm injection, pre-implantation genetic diagnosis, and sperm sorting for sex selection very shortly after they have been developed.

Research has stopped in promising areas of ART only when the Feds decide to get involved. For example, New Jersey Institute of Reproductive Medicine and Science researchers pioneered cytoplasmic transfer from donor eggs into the eggs of women that suffered from a defect in their cytoplasm. Revitalized, the eggs were fertilized, inserted into their mothers' wombs, and brought to term. Twenty children were born by means of the procedure, and then the FDA banned it. Cytoplasmic transfer is now available at fertility clinics in other countries. The latest breakthrough is in vitro maturation of eggs. Immature eggs are removed from a woman's ovaries and matured in a laboratory outside her body. This means that women no longer have to undergo uncomfortable hormone treatments to produce superovulation in order to obtain the number of eggs suitable for IVF procedures.

Meanwhile where federal research funding is most lavish and regulation is most onerous, that is where progress in getting treatments to patients is slowing down. The FDA approved only 18 new drugs in 2006, down from an average of 26 per year over the past six years. As the costs for getting through the regulatory gauntlet go up, pharmaceutical companies are narrowing their product lines and bringing fewer treatments to patients.

It is a truism among academic researchers and many economists that federal funding is necessary for basic research and that such funding is perpetually inadequate. However, a 2001 study by Organization for Economic Co-operation and Development [OECD] researchers found that in fact that higher spending by industry on R&D [research and development] correlates nicely with higher economic growth rates. In contrast to the academic truisms about the need for federal funding, the study found that "business-performed R&D ... drives the positive association between total R&D intensity and output growth."

Economic Growth Depends on Private-Sector Research Funding

The OECD researchers noted that publicly funded defense research actually crowded out private research, "while civilian public research is neutral with respect to business-performed R&D." In other words, government funded civilian research didn't hurt [the] private sector but there wasn't much evidence that it helped, at least in the short term. The report concluded, "Research and development activities undertaken by the business sector seem to have high social returns, while no clear-cut relationship could be established between non-business-oriented R&D activities and growth." In other words, economic growth was associated almost entirely with private sector research funding. The OECD report did allow that per-

Periodical Bibliography

The following articles have been selected to supplement the diverse views presented in this chapter.

America	"Cardinal Praises Bush for Stem Cell Veto," July 16, 2007.
P. Barry	"Female Stem Cells Flourish: Sex Difference Could Affect Therapies," *Science News*, April 14, 2007.
Richard Brookhiser	"Matters of Morality," *Time*, August 6, 2007.
Chap Clark	"Stem Cell Choices: What Does It Mean to Use Life to Give Life?" *Sojourners Magazine*, April 2007.
Kenneth Cooper	"A Beautiful Mind," *Essence*, July 2007.
Jet	"Stem Cell Testimony," April 30, 2007.
Sarah Kliff	"A Stem-Cell Surprise," *Newsweek*, July 30, 2007.
Katherine Leitzell	"A New Source for Stem Cells?" *U.S. News & World Report*, June 18, 2007.
David Nather	"Facing a Hard Sell on Stem Cells," *CQ Weekly*, March 19, 2007.
National Right to Life News	"Survivors Speak Out: Adult Stem Cells Save Lives," July 2007.
Rosemary Radford Ruether	"A Consistent Life Ethic? Supporting Life After Birth," *Conscience*, Spring 2007.
Jessica Ruvinsky	"Babies from Bone Marrow," *Discover*, July 2007.
Doug Trapp	"July 9, 2007: Bush Rejects Second Stem Cell Bill," *American Medical News*, July 9, 2007.

OPPOSING
VIEWPOINTS®
SERIES

CHAPTER 2

What Ethics Should Guide Reproductive Technology?

Chapter Preface

On July 25, 1978, headlines across the globe announced the news: Louise Brown, the first so-called "test-tube" baby, had been born. The day marked a milestone in reproductive technology by proving that human embryos that are fertilized outside of the womb can become viable human beings. Using a new procedure called "in vitro fertilization" (IFV), doctors brought hope to infertile couples. John and Leslie Brown, parents of Louise, had tried for nine years to have a child. When they consented to try IFV as a last resort, they ended up making history. Little Louise Brown became an instant celebrity in her hometown of Manchester, England, and beyond.

The IFV birth was the product of 12 years of research by Dr. Robert Edwards and Dr. Patrick Steptoe, two British scientists who pioneered IVF. The IVF process starts by retrieving the eggs from the mother and mixing them in the lab with sperm from the father. The resulting embryo is then placed back into the mother's uterus to develop normally until delivery. IVF is usually the treatment of choice for a woman with blocked or absent fallopian tubes, the very problem that Leslie Brown had. Initially, IVF only promised a 3 to 6 percent chance of leading to pregnancy. In the years after Louise's birth, however, medical developments brought the success rate up to an average of 23 percent, and even around 43 percent for women under thirty-five years of age. In the early 2000s, IVF is a popular choice for millions of infertile couples today.

Louise Brown's birth did not take place free of controversy. The Roman Catholic Church registered stringent objections on several levels. Since in vitro fertilization takes place outside of the body, the Church believed the procedure to be unnatural and sacrilegious. Moreover, the Church condemned IVF because a number of embryos are discarded, causing them to die during the process. In Catholic belief, embryos are human lives that should be protected like any other human beings. Others object to the high cost of IVF that therefore limits access to the infertility treatment only to those with substantial financial resources. Still others worry that IVF turns babies into commodities that can be bought and sold. These controversies and more resurface each time a new form of reproductive technology is developed and then offered to the public. In vitro fertilization may no longer be a shockingly new discovery to most people, but it still generates heated debate about what ethics should guide conception, pregnancy, and birth.

> *"Human cloning constitutes unethical experimentation. . . . It represents a giant step toward turning procreation into manufacture."*

Human Cloning Is Unethical

Leon Kass

There are two controversial kinds of human cloning research: reproductive (cloning to produce children) and therapeutic (cloning to study cell development to treat or avoid illness). Both involve the creation of embryos that are genetically identical. In the following viewpoint, bioethicist, biochemist, and physician Leon Kass calls both kinds of human cloning unethical, as an immoral violation of human identity and dignity and as a technology that would be impossible to limit or regulate. Leon Kass is the Addie Clark Harding Professor in the Committee on Social Thought at the University of Chicago and a fellow of the American Enterprise Institute, a conservative think tank in Washington, D.C. From 2002 to 2005 he was chairman of the President's Council on Bioethics under George W. Bush.

Leon Kass, "Drawing the Line Between Ethical Regenerative Medicine Research and Immoral Human Reproductive Cloning," testimony before the U.S. Senate Committee on the Judiciary, March 19, 2003, http://judiciary.senate.gov.

As you read, consider the following questions:

1. In the author's opinion, why would a law that banned reproductive cloning but allowed cloning for biomedical research be ineffective and unenforceable?

2. According to Kass, why would allowing research on five-to-six-day-old embryos lead to unethical research on fetuses at more advanced stages of development?

3. What other cells should be used instead of cloned embryos in biomedical research, in Kass's opinion?

Human cloning is immoral. . . . Human cloning constitutes unethical experimentation on the cloned-child-to-be. It confounds his genetic and social identity; it would threaten his sense of individuality. It represents a giant step toward turning procreation into manufacture. And it is a despotic attempt of parents to select and control the genetic make-up of their children. For all these reasons, I conclude that human cloning threatens the dignity of human procreation, giving one generation unprecedented control over the next, and marking a major step toward a eugenic world in which children would become objects of manipulation and products of will. Human cloning should be banned. . . .

Whether undertaken for the ultimate purpose of producing children or for the purpose of extracting stem cells for research, the deed of nuclear transplantation is itself an act of cloning (it is the deed that produces the genetic replica), and its product is in both cases identical: a cloned human embryo. This is the view of both the earlier National Bioethics Advisory Commission and the 2003 President's Council on Bioethics—including those members who favor cloning-for-biomedical-research—which unanimously adopted this terminology as accurate and fair. When identical cloned embryos are grown to the blastocyst stage, their different fates depend solely on the purposes of the human users: baby-making or research. The National Academy of Science report on Scientific and Medical Aspects of Human Reproductive Cloning (January 2002) also shares this opinion. . . .

Here then are my reasons for believing that a ban that tried to block cloning-to-produce children while permitting cloning-for-biomedical research is a bad idea and for supporting a comprehensive ban on all human cloning.

Stop the Process Before It Starts

Ineffective and counterproductive. If we want to prevent the development of anthrax bombs, we do best to block the production of anthrax spores, not just their transfer to a weapons delivery system. Similarly, if we mean to be fully serious about stopping the cloning of human children, we should try to stop the process before it starts, at the creation of the embryonic human clones, not merely rely on efforts to prevent their transfer to women for delivery. [A] law that tried to prevent cloning babies by banning only implantation of cloned embryos would be ineffective and unenforceable. It would be difficult to know when the law had been violated; it would be impossible to enforce it once it had [been violated]. Further, by endorsing cloning-for-research, such a law would in fact increase the likelihood of cloning-to-produce-children, by perfecting the procedure to practice it.

Permitting cloning for research will lead to improvement of cloning technique and increased success at getting cloned human embryos to the blastocyst stage, in the process making the whole practice safer. Once embryo-cloning techniques are thus perfected, people interested in cloning babies will be better able to succeed.

Once cloned embryos are produced and available in commercial laboratories, it will be very difficult to control what is done with them. As with the left-over embryos in the IVF

Therapeutic Human Cloning Is Slavery Plus Abortion

Cloning is an evil; and cloning for the purpose of research actually exacerbates the evil by countenancing the willful destruction of nascent human life. Moreover, it proposes doing this on a mass scale, as an institutionalized and routinized undertaking to extract medical benefits for those who have greater power. It is slavery plus abortion.

Diana Schaub, "A House Divided: Human Cloning"
Public Interest, *Winter 2003.*

clinics, cloned embryos produced for one purpose (research) could easily be used for another purpose (producing children).

Produced under conditions of industrial secrecy, they could be bought and sold without anyone's knowledge. Only under strict and transparent regulatory system of licensing, inventory, and reporting arrangements would we even have a guess as to the number and disposition of the cloned embryos produced.

Once available to medical practitioners of assisted reproduction, cloned embryos could be transferred to a woman's uterus without anyone's knowledge, protected by doctor-patient privacy and confidentiality.

Illicit "cloning pregnancies" would be impossible to detect.

Even if detected, there would be no enforceable legal remedy; the state could not and would not compel the abortion of the clone.

Use of Cloned Embryos Will Be Impossible to Limit

Ethically problematic. Allowing cloned embryos to be produced for biomedical research and/or stem cell extraction is morally highly problematic. It crosses several important moral boundaries, accelerating our slide down a slippery slope (or, more accurately, jumping us off an ethical cliff) into a dehumanizing world of genetic control of offspring and the routine use of nascent human life as a mere natural resource. In contrast, a ban on all human cloning is morally unproblematic.

[A] partial cloning ban crosses a major moral boundary by endorsing the deliberate production of early human embryos for the sole purpose of research and exploitation, and requiring their necessary destruction. (This goes beyond the use of the spare embryos in the IVF clinics, each one of which was created solely for reproductive use but is now no longer needed and will likely die anyhow. Only yesterday, in the stem cell debate of 2001, many proponents of embryonic stem cell research, made clear public statements opposing on moral grounds the creation of embryos specifically for research. Today they would cross that line without blinking. The slippery slope seems to be very steep.)

Cloned human embryos would be the first human embryos whose genetic makeup would be determined not by the chance union of egg and sperm but by deliberate human selection and design. When research cloning is seen in the context of growing powers of genetic screening and genetic manipulation of nascent human life, it becomes clear that saying 'yes' to creating cloned embryos, even for research, means saying 'yes,' at least in principle, to an ever-expanding genetic mastery of one generation over the next.

Use of cloned embryos in research, once allowed, will be impossible to limit. Arguments now used [as of 2003] to justify creating cloned embryos to produce stem cells also justify growing embryos beyond the blastocyst stage. Today the demand is for stem cells; tomorrow it will be for embryonic and fetal organs. Experiments with cloned cow embryos implanted in a cow's uterus (Advanced Cell Technologies) already suggest that there may be greater therapeutic potential using differentiated tissues (e.g., kidney primordia) harvested from early fetuses than using undifferentiated stem cells taken from the 5–6-day-old blastocyst stage. Should this prove correct, there will be great pressure to grow cloned human blastocysts to later stages, past 14 days—either in the uteruses (or other body cavities) of suitably prepared animal or human hosts or (eventually) using artificial placenta-like structures in the laboratory—in order to obtain the more useful tissues.

Combined with a legal prohibition on the implantation of cloned embryos (for the purpose of baby-making), permission to clone embryos for research creates a class of human embryos that it would be a federal felony not to destroy. Such a law obliges the state to enforce the destruction of nascent life, a troubling novelty.

In addition to the harm done to embryos, there is moral harm done to a society that comes to accept as normal the routinized production and use of early human life as a natural resource for our own benefit: we risk becoming desensitized, indifferent, callous; we lose our awe and respect for the mystery and wonder of emerging new human life.

Patenting and Selling Embryos Could Follow

Inadequate regulation [in proposed laws addressing cloned embryos].

They do not clearly apply to privately funded research.

They do not provide mechanisms for keeping track of all cloned embryos produced in laboratories, nor do they establish standards or guidelines for the handling and use of cloned human embryos.

They are silent on whether cloned human embryos can be patented.

They are silent on putting human nuclei into animal eggs. (The definitions of "oocyte" and "nuclear transplantation" offered in the bill do not specify that the egg be a human egg.)

The prohibition on "valuable consideration" for egg donation is effectively undermined by permitting compensation for time, costs, and inconvenience, absent declaring who gets to define those things, or how much is too much to charge. As written, the loophole swallows the rule and egg-selling is allowed to continue (as it does today in obtaining "donor" eggs for assisted reproduction). . . .

Cloning Is Not Essential for Basic Research

Unnecessary for promoting regenerative medicine research. The benefits of embryonic stem cell research (in both knowledge and potential therapy) do not necessarily require the creation of cloned embryos (or stem cells from cloned embryos). The putative benefits of cloning research are at best speculative, and it is unlikely to be the solution for the immune rejection problem. In contrast, a narrowly constructed yet complete ban on all human cloning would not interfere with stem cell research, adult or embryonic (using cells derived from non-cloned embryos).

The highly touted concept of "therapeutic cloning"—individualized, custom-made, rejection-proof cells derived from stem cells extracted from one's own embryonic clone—is not likely to succeed as an effective or practical form of regenerative medicine. Its alleged promise is vastly overrated, not to say spurious. . . .

There are other routes to solving the immune-rejection problem. Scientists are pursuing ways to engineer embryonic stem cells to make them rejection-proof in ALL recipients. Many new kinds of multipotent cells (found in the bone marrow, blood, fat, etc., of adults) have been transformed into nerve cells, bone cells, heart muscle cells, etc. If reintroduced into the patient from whose body they were first taken, these cells and tissues would not be rejected because they would contain only the patient's own DNA.

Cloning is not essential for basic research on selected diseases. If taken from patients with certain inherited diseases (e.g., juvenile diabetes), the multipotent adult precursor cells could be used to study the embryological development that leads to the diseases. It is not true that embryo cloning is the only way to obtain a library of stem cells that would permit such investigations.

Neither is it true that cloning of human embryos provides the only route to study the process of reprogramming of a specialized nucleus back to the unspecialized and totipotent state. Such studies can be carried out using somatic cell nuclear transfer in animals, with animal oocytes and animal donor somatic nuclei. They have yet to be done.

In sum: Even if no single argument above is by itself decisive, their cumulative weight leads me to support a comprehensive ban on all human cloning, including the cloning of embryos for research. Such a ban is prudent, moral, and virtually cost-free. It is the only real ban on human cloning. In contrast, a ban only on implanting cloned embryos is imprudent and morally dubious, and would likely yield little benefit that cannot be obtained by other (morally unproblematic) means. Purporting to be a ban on reproductive cloning, it would in fact increase the chances that cloned human beings would be born, and sooner rather than later.

> "[I] propose that scientists may one day grow cloned human embryos to term to prevent the suffering caused by hereditary disease."

Therapeutic Human Cloning Is Ethical

Ian Wilmut and Roger Highfield

English embryologist Ian Wilmut drew worldwide attention in 1997 when his team of researchers at the Roslin Institute in Scotland produced the world's first mammal cloned from adult cells, a sheep named Dolly who lived until 2003. In the following viewpoint, Wilmut and science journalist Roger Highfield argue that it is ethical to extend cloning technology to human embryos, not only to derive treatments to repair a person's own body but someday to correct hereditary defects at the embryo stage, which would allow the clone to develop into a healthy individual. Wilmut and Highfield insist that "environment, luck, and circumstance" determine personal identity, so it is impossible for cloning to produce an exact copy of a human being, even if their genes are identical. Ian Wilmut is the director of the Centre for

Regenerative Medicine at the University of Edinburgh. Roger Highfield is the science editor of the Daily Telegraph *in Britain.*

As you read, consider the following questions:

1. What degenerative diseases does human therapeutic cloning have a high potential of treating and even curing, according to Wilmut and Highfield?
2. Dolly the sheep was cloned from a ewe's body cells, not from a fertilized egg cell. How does the authors' qualified proposal to clone human beings differ from the way Dolly was cloned?
3. According to the authors, how do identical twins prove that no cloned human can be a copy of another human? What examples of cloned animals show that cloned individuals may not even look alike?

The life of Dolly opened up thrilling new opportunities in medicine and, by the same token, raised serious ethical issues and stirred many concerns. And continues to do so. . . .

I believe in the right to protest [human cloning]. I believe equally that right-wing religious paranoia is slowing the quest for treatments and, as a result, will harm people and cause suffering. I find it a constant cause of frustration that, in all the public debate, the harm that can be done to future generations by neglecting a useful technology is rarely taken into account. Disregarding the hype, of which there is much, I have no doubt about the long-term potential. The creation of cloned embryos from patients will, over the next few decades, lead to treatments for degenerative diseases such as heart disease, spinal cord injury, liver damage, diabetes, Parkinson's, motor neuron disease, and Alzheimer's—all of which cause damage to cells that, subsequently, are not repaired or replaced. By creating a cloned embryo of a patient, we can obtain a source of the patient's own cells—stem cells—that can be used to understand the disease, test treatments, and not only repair a body but regenerate it too. They can metamorphose into any cell type.

Cloning Should Be Allowed for Medical Treatments

We cannot know yet which of these serious diseases will be treated with cells from cloned embryos or when treatment will begin, but I believe that the drive to perfect them is strong because there is no fully effective treatment for any of them and in some cases there is none at all. One day doctors will be able to use cloning to grow a patient's own cells and tissues to carry out repairs. Cells from these embryos will also speed the search for the next generation of blockbuster medicines and help reduce our dependence on animal research. As a bonus, this work will give profound insights into human development and how it can go wrong and into how to correct many terrible genetic diseases in the embryo.

The potential of cloning to alleviate suffering—even end it for some diseases—is so great in the medium term that I believe it would be immoral not to clone human embryos for treatments. In the long term, a vast range of alternative and embryo-free ways to grow cells and tissues, perhaps even organs, may also rest on the foundations of this research. Cloning may by then have been a mere diversion that will eventually be superfluous.

Cloning Should Be Allowed to Correct Genetic Defects

However, I want to go even further than this and propose that scientists may one day grow cloned human embryos to term to prevent the suffering caused by hereditary disease. Doctors should be able to offer at-risk couples the opportunity to conceive with IVF [in vitro fertilization] methods, break down the resulting embryos into cells, correct any serious, genetic defects in these cells, and then clone demonstrably healthy cells to create a new embryo that can be implanted to start a pregnancy.

This does add up to a qualified proposal to clone and genetically alter human beings, but I hope to build a case to show that this approach could eventually be justified because it does not, paradoxically, entail cloning a person (by the understanding of most people) and because it could do much to combat serious genetic disease and to reduce human suffering.

My vision raises many technical questions. Scientists still have much to do to understand the process of cloning and the detailed molecular mechanisms of how it goes wrong and why it does so often. Only then will they find ways to make the process of cloning safe. Only then will they have complete confidence in growing a patient's cells, by the creation of embryo clones. Only then can they consider my proposal that for certain diseases we carry out the cloning of IVF embryos.

My vision faces stiff opposition. Many people will fight *any* proposal to create embryos. Many will object to *any* use of embryos in research. Many will object to *any* proposal to alter the genes of human beings. Many more besides are likely to feel profound unease at what I suggest. But I feel it is best to say what I think, rather than what people would like to hear, even though I suspect my peers will consider me at best brave, at worst foolhardy and naïve. Until now, it has been difficult to discuss these ideas in public. The drizzle of outlandish remarks and claims from the mavericks who say they are about to clone babies has distorted the media debate and fueled political efforts to ban all forms of cloning, both reproductive and therapeutic. In short, it has threatened to derail serious science. . . .

At the heart of the discomfort with my proposal is the status of the human embryo and whether it counts as a full version of human life or lies somewhere between the status of a cell and that of a person. Even if one accepts this gray scale of

The Political Agenda of Cloning Opponents

An alliance of abortion opponents, social conservatives, and biotechnology-phobes wants you to believe that human cloning is always unethical, even when it's done for the purpose of finding cures for horrible diseases. It isn't. . . .

There is so much confusion and misunderstanding surrounding cloning in part because it's tied to our ongoing battle over abortion. Abortion opponents continue to look for any opportunity to secure legal recognition for the personhood of an embryo. When abortion foes like President [George W.] Bush call for a ban on cloning, they are really using cloning as a tool to try to pry open *Roe v. Wade* [the 1973 Supreme Court decision that legalized abortion]. By claiming that cloned embryos are people and that their destruction has to be outlawed, they hope to get legal standing for all embryos. A ban on all forms of cloning would lead to bans on the destruction of all human embryos, cloned or otherwise. That would likely spell the end of abortion as well as in vitro fertilization and most forms of prenatal genetic testing in the United States.

Arthur Caplan,
"Cloning Ethics: Separating the Science from the Fiction,"
MSNBC.com, December 14, 2003.

life (and many people do not), does the embryo still deserve respect? And if it deserves respect, would that prohibit its use in research? Do the ends—new treatments for horrific diseases—always justify the means? There are broader questions raised by my agenda. What do we mean when we condemn research as unnatural? What do we actually mean by a human life and a person?. . .

Clones Will Never Be Copies

There are also good scientific reasons why clones will never be copies. Genes are not as powerful as many people think. A clone may have identical genes to those of the lost child, but that is not enough to ensure he develops the same way. The influence of genes is modified significantly by that of the environment. Genes are in constant dialogue with their surroundings. They are in dialogue with the rest of the cell in which they reside, which is in dialogue with other cells in the body, which in turn is in dialogue with the world at large, through education and experience. This nested dialogue shapes the development of a fertilized egg into brains or brawn. Just as one can never really relive a moment, this dialogue can never be exactly reproduced. As I explain below, the personality of a clone will be individual. Cloning cannot resurrect a loved one for this reason alone.

Many of the psychological burdens of cloning arise because many people still think—wrongly—that cloning offers a way to copy another human being, just as a photocopier duplicates a document. They imagine that the process of cloning would seek to capture not just a person but a person at a particular moment in time, perhaps even to go back to a lost moment, to try to defy what the novelist Milan Kundera called the unbearable lightness of being. This cannot be done: even identical twins who have developed in the same womb and experience the same upbringing are never really identical. Genetic identity is not the same as personal identity, and selves, unlike cells, cannot be cloned.

Because of the influence of environment, luck, and circumstance, it is impossible that my clone could grow up the same way as [I did]. He would grow up in a different time, in a different place, eating different food, hearing a language decorated with different slang and idiom. He would have different best friends, different teachers, different lovers, and so on. Take two people, one of whom spent her formative years in the postwar austerity of the 1940s and the other in the relatively well-off and liberal years of the twenty-first century. They could not possibly think alike.

Parents of natural clones—identical twins who have come from the same human egg—often dress them differently and emphasize differences in character in a bid to make them true individuals. This may be helpful for the twins, and their friends and family, but is unnecessary. From the very start of life, each embryo would have implanted in different places in the uterus, or drawn on different parts of the same placenta. As a consequence, they would have different access to food as well as different exposures to toxins and infections. They may start off with the same genetic code, but this can suffer different errors and mistakes as genes multiply in their bodies. The way genes are turned on and off by a process called imprinting can be patchy and vary between twins. Slight differences in the frequency of cell division or the rate of cell migration may slightly alter the appearance of one twin relative to the other.

The brain would be affected in a similar way. Small changes in the way the nervous system wires up and matures might also influence ability or behavior, although many other factors will be important as well in determining these characteristics. Identical twins are more similar than you and I are. But they are not really identical at all.

Plenty of evidence from animal cloning, from cats to mules, shows how environment shapes an individual as much as genes do. We cloned a quartet of young Dorset rams, Cedric, Cyril, Cecil, and Tuppence, from embryo cells that had been grown (cultured) in the laboratory. They were genetically identical to the same culture of Poll Dorset embryo cells and yet were very different in size and temperament. Although they were all more aggressive than females, as one would expect, Tuppence was by far the quietest of the four. Small variations in cell division and migration result in differences in the pattern of black-and-white skin in Holstein dairy cattle. The world's first cloned horse—Prometa, unveiled in 2003 by Cesare Galli of the Laboratory of Reproductive Technologies, Cremona, Italy—could be distinguished from her sister/ mother (unusually, she was the clone of the horse that carried her) by a white stripe. And so on.

As variation is to be expected in any species, pet owners should not expect clones of Tiddles to be identical to their late lamented cat. This was observed with the first feline clones, created at Texas A&M by Mark Westhusin. Rainbow the cat was a typical calico with splotches of brown, tan, and gold on white. Cc (carbon copy), her clone, had a stripy gray coat over white. And while Rainbow was chunky, Cc was sleek; Rainbow was reserved, Cc was playful; and so on. The prospects of making exact copies of Patch the cat and Spot the dog look bleak.

"In almost every case, the religious debate [on cloning] is still open-ended."

There Is No Religious Consensus on the Ethics of Human Cloning

Bob Sullivan

The cloning debate is often portrayed in science-versus-religion terms, but, as investigative reporter Bob Sullivan demonstrates in the following viewpoint, this presumed divide is too simplistic. Among the world's religions there is considerable disagreement over the ethics of human cloning: According to Sullivan, conservative Christians categorically oppose all cloning, Jewish beliefs permit therapeutic human cloning, Buddhist tradition has no stated position, and Hindu and Muslim scholars variously voice strong objections and cautious approval of cloning. Ultimately, Sullivan argues, people's support for or opposition to cloning is not based on religious beliefs. Bob Sullivan is a senior technology writer for MSNBC.com, specializing in computer crime and Internet privacy issues.

Bob Sullivan, "Beyond Dolly, The History of Cloning: Religions Reveal Little Consensus on Cloning," *MSNBC.com*, August 16, 2002. Republished with permission of MSNBC, conveyed through Copyright Clearance Center, Inc.

As you read, consider the following questions:

1. According to Damien Keown, cited by Sullivan, what Buddhist teachings can be interpreted to allow human cloning?

2. On what bases do some Muslim scholars oppose cloning and others approve of the technology, according to the author?

3. What poll results lead Sullivan to conclude that Americans do not base their opinion of human cloning on religious beliefs?

A confused population looking for clear ethical wisdom on cloning might be disappointed: Beyond issuing a general call for caution, the world's spiritual leaders hardly speak with one voice on the cloning debate.

What would Jesus do? Or Buddha? Or the Dalai Lama? The announcement of sheep-clone Dolly in 1997 sent many religious leaders to the pulpit. Others scrambled through religious texts looking for guidance. There were plenty of swift condemnations.

But as the realities and limitations of science have removed some of the haze surrounding cloning, the philosophical and religious debates have also come into focus.

Today [as of 2002], conservative Christians are still unmoved from their blanket opposition to all cloning. Other faiths have found room in their traditions for therapeutic cloning—the use of cloned cells for research and health reasons, but not for breeding humans. Some even find ethical room for the cloning of humans.

But in almost every case, the religious debate is still open-ended. Other than opposition to the more sinister possibilities, such as the creation of "spare-parts" humans, there is hardly consensus about the ethics of cloning. In the absence of a central teaching authority, akin to the Roman Catholic Church's Congregation for the Doctrine of the Faith, many religious scholars are still openly debating the pros and cons of a powerful new science that could bring as much potential for hope as for horror.

Three Basic Questions

The discussion eventually wraps itself around three central questions: Would cloning somehow corrupt traditional family relationships and lineage? Is destruction of a fertilized embryo during research murder? And perhaps more fundamentally, does cloning meddle with God's universe in a way that humans shouldn't?

Picking a position on cloning is actually an exercise in revisiting basic religious beliefs, says Courtney Campbell, director of the Program for Ethics, Science and the Environment at Oregon State University.

For example, most Jews and Muslims don't consider a fertilized embryo to have full human status, which essentially gives a green light to therapeutic cloning research. In that sense, the discussion about therapeutic cloning tends to follow lines similar to the debate over stem cell research and, ultimately, abortion.

"Thinking about cloning ought to require traditions to go back and think through basic tenets, such as does life really begin at conception," Campbell said. "You can't avoid that question."

To most faithful, answering such deep questions requires study of religious texts. Some people might think thousand-year-old writings would offer little guidance on 21st-century scientific morality, but that's not true, says Rabbi Edward Reichman, assistant professor of philosophy and history at Yeshiva University Einstein College of Medicine.

"The (Jewish) law is relevant to any imaginable technology," he said. "When you apply the law to a new technology, you can seek direct precedent, or you can . . . seek to distill a principle of the law that applies.

"With evolution, Darwin, Copernicus, it was fundamentally the same. It was an unknown thing one couldn't have dreamed of when the law was written, but where the principles applied."

Jewish law is squarely on the side of medical research that has potential to save and preserve life, Reichman said. As a result, Jewish scholars are generally among the most vocal religious leaders in support of therapeutic cloning.

"The Jewish faith generally welcomes new technologies and sciences in as much as they can benefit the world, especially medicine. We do not necessarily perceive all advances as stepping on God's toes," he said.

Red Light, Green Light

But that's exactly the interpretation arrived at by Roman Catholic scholars after examining the Bible and Canon Law. Back in 1987, the church became the leading voice against human cloning of any kind. In a document called "Donum Vitae," Roman Catholics were told that cloning was "considered contrary to the moral law, since (it is in) opposition to the dignity both of human procreation and of the conjugal union."

The church still holds that position, which is also supported by conservative Christians such as Southern Baptists. However, there is great diversity of opinion among other Christian denominations, and even within those denominations.

Oregon State's Campbell compiled the most comprehensive look at religious perspectives in 1997, for the National Bioethics Advisory Commission appointed by then-President Bill Clinton.

Campbell used a simple traffic-light system to classify the religious points of view: Catholics and Southern Baptists issue clear red lights on both therapeutic and human cloning. But among "mainline" Protestants such as the Lutheran and Episcopal faiths, Campbell found some green and yellow lights.

African American and Native American Religious Views of Cloning

Animal cloning and human cloning both risk substantial disruption of the created order and balance in nature, according to some Native American views. Animal cloning is seen as eroding the reverence and kinship between humans and other created beings. "We are becoming more like Creator every day ... however, it is only our abilities that are growing that way," says Muskogee tribe elder Sakim. ... "We are not blessed with nor in any manner fraught with the judgment of Creator. That is the fundamental problem." However, some support for human cloning can be found among Native Americans who are worried about the preservation of endangered indigenous peoples and see cloning as a possible way to ensure survival.

Most African-American churches—which stem largely from Methodist and Baptist traditions—affirm that life begins at conception, which leaves little room for any embryonic research. Black churches are also sensitive to the potential abuses minorities may face in the name of medical research because of incidents like the Tuskegee experiments from 1932 to 1972 in which African-Americans were denied syphilis treatments.

Courtney Campbell, "Religious Views on Cloning: Cloning Human Beings," MSNBC.com, August 16, 2002.

"Some traditions and leading figures in conservative Protestantism who were opposed to human cloning for reproductive reasons have come to see that given the ambiguity about their own views about the status of embryonic life, and given the potential for health benefits, they could be opposed to reproductive cloning, but affirm therapeutic cloning," Campbell said. The main reason, Campbell says, is the tradition of emphasizing individual choice over central dogma.

Buddhism: Yes and No

Some other faiths are even harder to pin down. For example, there is no stated position among Buddhists on cloning, so scholars like Campbell are left only to interpret the tradition's precepts on their own.

Buddhism might be willing to accept cloning, Campbell said, because it represents a leap in modern science and self-understanding that could be considered a path to enlightenment. On the other hand, the Eightfold Path prohibits harm to any sentient beings, which could be seen in the destruction of cells necessary to perform cloning research. Campbell's judgment: a yellow light on the issues raised by human cloning, and a flashing red light on other implications of cloning research.

Damien Keown, professor at Goldsmiths College in London and perhaps the best-known expert on possible Buddhist responses to cloning, generally agreed. He said the tradition doesn't have the same kind of fundamental moral opposition that can be found in Christian faiths. Buddhists already believe in non-sexual reproduction, for example, since Buddhism teaches that life can come into being through supernatural phenomenon like spontaneous generation. "Life can thus legitimately begin in more ways than one," he said.

"For Christians, to bring into being a new human or animal life by cloning as opposed to normal sexual reproduction is to 'play God' and usurp the power of the creator. This is not a problem for Buddhism, because in Buddhism the creation of new life is not seen as a 'gift from God,'" Keown said. "For this reason the technique in itself would not be seen as problematic."

Buddhism sees human individuality as a mirage, so adherents wouldn't share some of the other philosophical complaints that Western thinkers have about cloning, as it pertains to devaluing an individual's personality or character by creating copies.

But that hardly means Buddhists will welcome clones. On more practical grounds, Buddhism promotes ultimate respect to every sentient being, and that generally includes cells born out of research. Destroying such cells, even in research on animal cloning, runs contrary to Buddhist teaching.

"It is hard to see what purposes—scientific or otherwise—can justify the dehumanization that results when life is created and manipulated for other ends," Keown said. "We should not forget that Ian Wilmut, the creator of Dolly, failed 276 times before Dolly was conceived."

Hindus, Muslims

Hindu religious scholars have issued flashing red lights, according to Campbell—which means they are calling for a temporary pause to provide time to think, but have not issued an outright objection or human cloning.

A Hindu's sense of the world and the relationship between people and Creator is very different from Western traditions, so Hindus also wouldn't have the same fundamental objection to "playing God" that Christians might. But there are plenty of concerns about the desire for greed and power that might be served by aggressive scientists who call for cloning.

Diversity among Muslims makes an authoritative description of Islamic thought on cloning nearly impossible. Dr. Abdulaziz Sachedina, University of Virginia professor and a leading U.S. scholar on Muslim thought regarding cloning, believes that most Muslims will eventually agree that scientists wouldn't have discovered cloning if Allah hadn't willed it. So cloning for the purpose of enhancing the chances of procreating within a solid family structure will be "regarded as an act of faith in the ultimate will of God as the Giver of all life."

But he's hardly without opponents. Nasser Farid Wasel, Egypt's Mufti, said in 1999 that cloning clearly contradicts Islam. Other muftis have gone further, saying scientists who clone are doing Satan's work.

Dr. Ibrahim B. Syed, director of the Islamic Research Foundation International and an outspoken cloning supporter, says such absolute statements from religious leaders only serve to complicate the conversation.

"Anything new, just as a reaction, they oppose it," Syed said. "Our religious leaders have little knowledge of evolving technologies." But the problem works both ways, he conceded. "The scientists don't know anything about religious beliefs, often."

Science vs. Religion

Scientific advances have shaken religious beliefs to their roots repeatedly through the ages. Charles Darwin did it. Copernicus did it. And now, companies like Advanced Cell Technologies are doing it.

But as much as religious leaders want to push scientists to think more about the morality of their work, scientists are pushing religious leaders back to the basic tenets of their faiths, where they scramble to make sense of a world teetering on the razor's edge of irreversible change.

While it might be a frightening moment, it's also a grand opportunity, Campbell said.

"Science can be a spur to creative and innovative theological thought," he said. "And I think what is a crying need is for the church to be a forum for discussion with engaged dialogue between science and religion, and be a venue for civic conversation."

In the debate over cloning, will religious views ultimately matter? Already, some scientists are working faster than ethicists on cloning. And at least in the United States, there is an open question about the weight given to religious leaders' opinions on cloning.

Four out of five people said they opposed cloning in a survey conducted [in 2001] for the Pew Forum on Religion and Public Life and the Pew Research Center for the People and the Press. But only one in four Catholics and one in three Protestants cited religious beliefs as the main reasons for their opposition. Pollsters say many Americans pride themselves on developing their own opinions rather than consulting religious dogma—which means that the key decisions on cloning are much more likely to be made in the House of Representatives than in a house of God.

> *"To appreciate children as gifts is to accept them as they come, not as objects of our design or products of our will or instruments of our ambition."*

The Selection of Offspring Traits Is Unethical

Michael J. Sandel

In the following viewpoint, philosophy professor Michael J. Sandel compares human genetic engineering for nonmedical purposes—not to treat disease but to select traits such as height, sex, and muscle strength—to the hubris of Prometheus, the mythological Greek rebel who set out to create humans in the gods' image (and was punished). Genetic enhancements, Sandel argues, are a much more troubling counterpart to modern society's obsession with cosmetic surgery and high-pressure child-rearing practices: All are attempts to master nature that undermine our appreciation of human achievement and our sense of life as a gift. Michael J. Sandel is Anne T. and Robert M. Bass Professor of Government at Harvard University and the author of The Case Against Perfection: Ethics in the Age of Genetic Engineering *(2007).*

Michael J. Sandel, "The Case Against Perfection," *Atlantic Monthly*, vol. 293, no. 3, April 2004, pp. 51–61. Copyright © 2004 Michael J. Sandel. Reproduced by permission of the author.

As you read, consider the following questions:

1. In Sandel's view, how would genetic enhancement corrupt the two most-admired aspects of athletic achievement, effort and giftedness?

2. According to the author, how is the relation between parent and child changed when a child's traits are genetically engineered?

3. In Sandel's opinion, why is eugenics morally objectionable whether it is state-coerced, as practiced by the Nazis, or freely chosen, as practiced by buyers of eggs and sperm when they select the genetic traits they desire?

Breakthroughs in genetics present us with a promise and a predicament. The promise is that we may soon be able to treat and prevent a host of debilitating diseases. The predicament is that our newfound genetic knowledge may also enable us to manipulate our own nature—to enhance our muscles, memories, and moods; to choose the sex, height, and other genetic traits of our children; to make ourselves "better than well." . . .

Like cosmetic surgery, genetic enhancement employs medical means for nonmedical ends—ends unrelated to curing or preventing disease or repairing injury. But unlike cosmetic surgery, genetic enhancement is more than skin-deep. If we are ambivalent about surgery or Botox injections for sagging chins and furrowed brows, we are all the more troubled by genetic engineering for stronger bodies, sharper memories, greater intelligence, and happier moods. The question is whether we are right to be troubled, and if so, on what grounds. . . .

Genetic Enhancement Demeans Both Effort and Giftedness

To acknowledge the giftedness of life is to recognize that our talents and powers are not wholly our own doing, despite the effort we expend to develop and to exercise them. It is also to recognize that not everything in the world is open to whatever use we may desire or devise. Appreciating the gifted quality of life constrains the Promethean project [the arrogant belief that humans can control, or are above, nature] and conduces to a certain humility. It is in part a religious sensibility. But its resonance reaches beyond religion.

It is difficult to account for what we admire about human activity and achievement without drawing upon some version of this idea. Consider two types of athletic achievement. We appreciate [baseball] players like Pete Rose, who are not blessed with great natural gifts but who manage, through striving, grit, and determination, to excel in their sport. But we also admire players like Joe DiMaggio, who display natural gifts with grace and effortlessness. Now, suppose we learned that both players took performance-enhancing drugs. Whose turn to drugs would we find more deeply disillusioning? Which aspect of the athletic ideal—effort or gift—would be more deeply offended?

Some might say effort: The problem with drugs is that they provide a shortcut, a way to win without striving. But striving is not the point of sports; excellence is. And excellence consists at least partly in the display of natural talents and gifts that are no doing of the athlete who possesses them. This is an uncomfortable fact for democratic societies. We want to believe that success, in sports and in life, is something we earn, not something we inherit. Natural gifts, and the admiration they inspire, embarrass the meritocratic faith; they cast doubt on the conviction that praise and rewards flow from effort alone. In the face of this embarrassment we inflate the moral significance of striving, and depreciate giftedness. This distortion can be seen, for example, in network-television coverage of the Olympics, which focuses less on the feats the athletes perform than on heartrending stories of the hardships they have overcome and the struggles they have waged to triumph over an injury or a difficult upbringing or political turmoil in their native land.

But effort isn't everything. No one believes that a mediocre basketball player who works and trains even harder than Michael Jordan deserves greater acclaim or a bigger contract. The real problem with genetically altered athletes is that they corrupt athletic competition as a human activity that honors the cultivation and display of natural talents. From this standpoint, enhancement can be seen as the ultimate expression of the ethic of effort and willfulness—a kind of high-tech striving. The ethic of willfulness and the biotechnological powers it now enlists are arrayed against the claims of giftedness.

Appreciating Children Involves Accepting Them as They Come

The ethic of giftedness, under siege in sports, persists in the practice of parenting. But here, too, bioengineering and genetic enhancement threaten to dislodge it. To appreciate children as gifts is to accept them as they come, not as objects of our design or products of our will or instruments of our ambition. Parental love is not contingent on the talents and attributes a child happens to have. We choose our friends and spouses at least partly on the basis of qualities we find attractive. But we do not choose our children. Their qualities are unpredictable, and even the most conscientious parents cannot be held wholly responsible for the kind of children they have. That is why parenthood, more than other human relationships, teaches what the theologian William F. May calls an "openness to the unbidden."

May's resonant phrase helps us see that the deepest moral objection to enhancement lies less in the perfection it seeks than in the human disposition it expresses and promotes. The problem is not that parents usurp the autonomy of a child they design. The problem lies in the hubris of the designing parents, in their drive to master the mystery of birth. Even if

A Biological Arms Race

Say you're perfectly happy with the prospect of a child who shares the unmodified genes of you and your partner. Say you think that manipulating the DNA of your child might be dangerous, or presumptuous, or icky? How long will you be able to hold that line if the procedure begins to spread among your neighbors? Maybe not so long as you think: If germline manipulation actually does begin, it seems likely to set off a kind of biological arms race. "Suppose parents could add thirty points to their child's IQ," asks MIT economist Lester Thurow. "Wouldn't you want to do it? And if you don't, your child will be the stupidest in the neighborhood." That's precisely what it might feel like to be the parent facing the choice. Individual competition more or less defines the society we've built, and in that context love can almost be defined as giving your kids what they need to make their way in the world. Deciding not to soup them up . . . well, it could come to seem like child abuse.

Of course, the problem about arms races is that you never really get anywhere. If everyone's adding thirty IQ points, then having an IQ of one hundred fifty won't get you any closer to Stanford than you were at the outset. The very first athlete engineered to use twice as much oxygen as the next guy will be unbeatable in the Tour de France—but in no time he'll merely be the new standard. You'll have to do what he did to be in the race, but your upgrades won't put you ahead, merely back on a level playing field. You might be able to argue that society as a whole was helped, because there was more total brainpower at work, but your kid won't be any closer to the top of the pack. All you'll be able to do is guarantee she won't be left hopelessly far behind.

Bill McKibben, "Designer Genes," Orion, May–June 2003.

this disposition did not make parents tyrants to their children, it would disfigure the relation between parent and child, and deprive the parent of the humility and enlarged human sympathies that an openness to the unbidden can cultivate. . . .

Some see a clear line between genetic enhancement and other ways that people seek improvement in their children and themselves. Genetic manipulation seems somehow worse—more intrusive, more sinister—than other ways of enhancing performance and seeking success. But morally speaking, the difference is less significant than it seems. Bioengineering gives us reason to question the low-tech, high-pressure child-rearing practices we commonly accept. The hyperparenting familiar in our time represents an anxious excess of mastery and dominion that misses the sense of life as a gift. This draws it disturbingly close to eugenics.

Call It What It Is: Eugenics

The shadow of eugenics hangs over today's debates about genetic engineering and enhancement. Critics of genetic engineering argue that human cloning, enhancement, and the quest for designer children are nothing more than "privatized" or "free-market" eugenics. Defenders of enhancement reply that genetic choices freely made are not really eugenic—at least not in the pejorative sense. To remove the coercion, they argue, is to remove the very thing that makes eugenic policies repugnant.

Sorting out the lesson of eugenics is another way of wrestling with the ethics of enhancement. The Nazis gave eugenics a bad name. But what, precisely, was wrong with it? Was the old eugenics objectionable only insofar as it was coercive? Or is there something inherently wrong with the resolve to deliberately design our progeny's traits?

James Watson, the biologist who, with Francis Crick, discovered the structure of DNA, sees nothing wrong with genetic engineering and enhancement, provided they are freely chosen rather than state-imposed. And yet Watson's language contains more than a whiff of the old eugenic sensibility. "If you really are stupid, I would call that a disease," he told the *Times* of London. "The lower 10 percent who really have diffi- culty, even in elementary school, what's the cause of it? A lot of people would like to say, 'Well, poverty, things like that.' It probably isn't. So I'd like to get rid of that, to help the lower 10 percent." A few years ago Watson stirred controversy by saying that if a gene for homosexuality were discovered, a woman should be free to abort a fetus that carried it. When his remark provoked an uproar, he replied that he was not singling out gays but asserting a principle: Women should be free to abort fetuses for any reason of genetic preference—for example, if the child would be dyslexic, or lacking musical tal- ent, or too short to play basketball.

Watson's scenarios are clearly objectionable to those for whom all abortion is an unspeakable crime. But for those who do not subscribe to the pro-life position, these scenarios raise a hard question: If it is morally troubling to contemplate abortion to avoid a gay child or a dyslexic one, doesn't this suggest that something is wrong with acting on any eugenic preference, even when no state coercion is involved?

Consider the market in eggs and sperm. The advent of ar- tificial insemination allows prospective parents to shop for ga- metes with the genetic traits they desire in their offspring. It is a less predictable way to design children than cloning or pre- implantation genetic screening, but it offers a good example of a procreative practice in which the old eugenics meets the new consumerism. A few years ago some Ivy League newspa- pers ran an ad seeking an egg from a woman who was at least five feet ten inches tall and athletic, had no major family medical problems, and had a combined SAT score of 1400 or above. The ad offered $50,000 for an egg from a donor with these traits. More recently [as of 2004] a Web site was launched claiming to auction eggs from fashion models whose photos appeared on the site, at starting bids of $15,000 to $150,000.

On what grounds, if any, is the egg market morally objectionable? Since no one is forced to buy or sell, it cannot be wrong for reasons of coercion. Some might worry that hefty prices would exploit poor women by presenting them with an offer they couldn't refuse. But the designer eggs that fetch the highest prices are likely to be sought from the privileged, not the poor. If the market for premium eggs gives us moral qualms, this, too, shows that concerns about eugenics are not put to rest by freedom of choice.

Marketing Sperm Is Equally Troubling

A tale of two sperm banks helps explain why. The Repository for Germinal Choice, one of America's first sperm banks, was not a commercial enterprise. It was opened in 1980 by Robert Graham, a philanthropist dedicated to improving the world's "germ plasm" and counteracting the rise of "retrograde humans." His plan was to collect the sperm of Nobel Prize–winning scientists and make it available to women of high intelligence, in hopes of breeding supersmart babies. But Graham had trouble persuading Nobel laureates to donate their sperm for his bizarre scheme, and so settled for sperm from young scientists of high promise. His sperm bank closed in 1999.

In contrast, California Cryobank, one of the world's leading sperm banks, is a for-profit company with no overt eugenic mission. Cappy Rothman, M.D., a co-founder of the firm, has nothing but disdain for Graham's eugenics, although the standards Cryobank imposes on the sperm it recruits are exacting. Cryobank has offices in Cambridge, Massachusetts, between Harvard and MIT, and in Palo Alto, California, near Stanford. It advertises for donors in campus newspapers (compensation up to $900 a month), and accepts less than five percent of the men who apply. Cryobank's marketing materials play up the prestigious source of its sperm. Its catalogue provides detailed information about the physical characteristics of each donor, along with his ethnic origin and college major. For an extra fee prospective customers can buy the results of a test that assesses the donor's temperament and character type. Rothman reports that Cryobank's ideal sperm donor is six feet tall, with brown eyes, blond hair, and dimples, and has a college degree—not because the company wants to propagate those traits, but because those are the traits his customers want: "If our customers wanted high school dropouts, we would give them high school dropouts."

Not everyone objects to marketing sperm. But anyone who is troubled by the eugenic aspect of the Nobel Prize sperm bank should be equally troubled by Cryobank, consumer-driven though it be. What, after all, is the moral difference between designing children according to an explicit eugenic purpose and designing children according to the dictates of the market? Whether the aim is to improve humanity's "germ plasm" or to cater to consumer preferences, both practices are eugenic insofar as both make children into products of deliberate design. . . .

There is something appealing, even intoxicating, about a vision of human freedom unfettered by the given. It may even be the case that the allure of that vision played a part in summoning the genomic age into being. It is often assumed that the powers of enhancement we now possess arose as an inadvertent by-product of biomedical progress—the genetic revolution came, so to speak, to cure disease, and stayed to tempt us with the prospect of enhancing our performance, designing our children, and perfecting our nature. That may have the story backwards. It is more plausible to view genetic engineering as the ultimate expression of our resolve to see ourselves astride the world, the masters of our nature. But that promise of mastery is flawed. It threatens to banish our appreciation of life as a gift, and to leave us with nothing to affirm or behold outside our own will.

> "If biological manipulation is indeed a slippery slope, then we are already sliding down that slope now and may as well enjoy the ride."

The Selection of Offspring Traits Is Inevitable

Gregory Stock

In the following viewpoint, biophysicist and science writer Gregory Stock argues that genetic enhancement technology is already in use; impossible to ban; and just as ethical, desirable, and needed as amniocentesis, vaccination, and many other controversial breakthroughs that disrupted the status quo. In Stock's opinion, the ethical approach to germinal choice technology is to accept its risks and explore it scientifically and above all openly. Openness, he maintains, will minimize problems, surprises, and abuses, but a ban will only drive the practice underground into the hands of rogue scientists and the black market. Gregory Stock is CEO of Signum Biosciences, a company developing treatments for Alzheimer's disease, and former director of the Program on Medicine, Technology, and Society at the UCLA School of Public Health.

As you read, consider the following questions:

1. Why does Stock argue that no ban can stop germinal choice technology from spreading?

2. According to Stock, what accepted practices already tamper with the human gene pool, and how might *not* tampering with a person's genetic makeup be considered unethical?

3. What bigger threats do we have to fear from totalitarian regimes than eugenic abuses, in the author's opinion?

One day we will manipulate the genes of our children in sophisticated ways using advanced germinal choice technologies. In spite of a general uneasiness about such technologies, we will likely use—and misuse—them as soon as they arrive, just as we have earlier breakthroughs along this path. Prospective parents use ultrasound to determine the gender of a fetus so they can abort a baby girl, amniocentesis to look for the telltale extra chromosome 21 of Down syndrome, preimplantation genetic diagnosis [PGD] to select an embryo free of cystic fibrosis. Single-cell diagnostics are still too rudimentary and expensive to make broad PGD screenings feasible, but the desire and the perceived need are clear. . . .

That we will halt the global scientific effort to elucidate human genetics is inconceivable. And we will have no trouble figuring out how to justify using more potent germinal choice technologies as they emerge. Bans in this or that country surely won't keep them from spreading. When large numbers of people want something that regulators cannot monitor and that small laboratories in any country can provide, people obtain it.

Though the prospect of genetic manipulation disturbs William Gardner, a bioethicist at the University of Pittsburgh, he argues convincingly that no ban can stop it:

Both nations and parents have strong incentives to defect from a ban on human genetic enhancement, because enhancements would help them in competitions with other parents and nations. The ban on enhancement, moreover, is vulnerable to even small defections because the disadvantages of defecting late will increase the incentives for non-defectors to follow suit, causing defections to cascade. . . .

The most difficult type of germinal choice technology for people to accept is germline enhancement—the direct manipulation of an embryo's genome to improve it in some way. . . .

Arguments against human germline enhancement rest largely on assertions that it is morally wrong, that it is too dangerous, that it will be badly abused, or that it could bring dire indirect consequences in personal, political, social, environmental, or spiritual ways. Let's look at each of these.

Challenging the Moral Argument

The most common form of the first assertion, that germline enhancement is morally wrong, is: we should not play God. But there are many secular variations. Along with our "right to unaltered genes" are the ideas that children should not be manufactured, that our gene pool is the common property of all humanity, and that genetic manipulation would assault human dignity.

As for playing God, by the measure of earlier ages, we do just that every time we give our children penicillin, use birth control, fly in an airplane, or telephone a friend. We embrace technologies that tame and harness nature because we think they improve our lives, and we will accept or reject human genetic manipulation on the same grounds.

But perhaps the scale of primitive humans is no longer appropriate, and playing God is a rather hyperbolic way of speaking about any of our tinkering with the natural world. At a 2001 conference on cloning, Rabbi Moses Tendler, a professor of Jewish medical ethics at Yeshiva University, spoke against reproductive cloning, but not because he considered it playing God:

> God gave us molecules. God gave us atoms. We put them together differently. We are not playing God by doing that. We can't get along without Him. . . . God is the source of all science and God is the source of religion, and God is not schizophrenic. He doesn't fight with Himself. If there is seemingly conflict between the two, it's based upon one of three possibilities. We don't understand what God said, we don't understand the science, or, the usual explanation, we don't understand either.

Metaphors about "human manufacturing" are another way of articulating that germline manipulation would somehow violate the natural order. The infusion of conscious human choice into the process of conceiving a child blurs the line between the biological and the technological in the same way that artificial intelligence does, but genetic engineering is not about to turn our children into manufactured products. A freely chosen nine-month pregnancy is nothing like the controlled and optimized assembly-line manufacturing evoked by this metaphor. Moreover, children, whatever their genetic makeup, are far too influenced by the vagaries of individual experience to be anything but unique and highly individual.

Communal ownership of the human gene pool is an even stranger concept. The gene pool is a conceptual abstraction that is simply the sum total of all the genes of the reproducing population. We affect the gene pool every time we save a diabetic who would otherwise die before reproducing, every time we bring a child into the world, every time we inoculate a child, protecting him or her from fatal infectious diseases. Do those who argue for collective control of our gene pool imagine that humanity as a whole should oversee these choices as well? Such invocations of the sanctity of our gene pool are not scientific but religious arguments. John Fletcher, who was the first chief of the bioethics program at the National Institutes of Health and is now professor emeritus of biomedical ethics at the University of Virginia, commented in 1998:

> The idea of natural law is one that I think is not a viable concept when it comes to the gene pool ... Suppose we really knew how to treat cystic fibrosis or some other very burdensome disease and didn't do it because of the belief that people had a right to an untampered genetic patrimony. Then, you met a person twenty-five years later and did the Golden Rule thing and said, "Well, you know, we could have treated you for this, but we wanted to respect your right to your untampered genetic patrimony. Sorry." It doesn't take a highfalutin ethicist to realize that's just plain wrong. You violate one of the basic principles of morality, namely that you want to treat a person as you would want to be treated.

The moral and religious arguments against genetic manipulation are unconvincing to me....

Challenging the Argument that Genetic Enhancement Is Too Difficult

The next assertion, that germline enhancement is too difficult and dangerous, is not a valid argument against exploring the technology. The complexity of the human genome is obvious to any geneticist. Six months after completion of its rough draft in June 2000, geneticists still disagreed about the total number of genes. Reports in early 2000 that there were only some 30,000 of them came as a shock to scientists who had thought there would be 100,000 or more. Not only do the influences of most of our genes depend on the nuances of the surrounding genetic background, many genes code for several different proteins. Some observers throw up their hands at this thicket and say that untangling our genome enough to be able to shape the traits of our children is fantasy. Others ad-mit the possibility, but believe that the dangers and uncertainties will always preclude safe germline manipulation in humans. . . .

If germline engineering never becomes safe enough for human use, this will pose little risk. Efforts to modify human embryos might still occasionally take place, but these failures would be a minor problem compared with the many thousands of instances of fetal damage from alcohol and drug abuse and trauma. Our failure in germline research might be a letdown to those who hope that medical science will enable us to transcend our biological limits, but previous generations have come to grips with these, and I daresay we could too. Many people would heave a sigh of relief knowing that science fiction would remain fiction, that human biology would remain the biology we know, and that the present whirlwind of change would not drag loose this anchor of our identity.

In short, if our science proves incapable of reworking human biology more deeply than will occur through embryo selection, no ban on germline engineering is needed. Only if such interventions offer a safe and reliable path toward a substantive enhancement of human traits—the addition of vital years to our lives or improved physical and mental functioning—will we face difficult decisions. Success, not failure, is what will force us to decide when to use this powerful tool and how to deal with its personal, social, and political consequences. . . .

Challenging the Argument that Genetic Enhancement Will Be Abused

The third assertion is that even if germline enhancement were beneficial in some ways, the technology would invite too much abuse. Critics who take this tack fear that the government will initiate eugenic programs to shape the genetics of its citizens. They worry that parents, perhaps seduced by advertisements or competitive pressures, will make dangerously mistaken

Choosing a Genetic Defect Can Be an Ethical Choice

Susannah A. Baruch and colleagues at the Genetics and Public Policy Center at Johns Hopkins University surveyed 190 American P.G.D. [preimplantation genetic diagnosis] clinics, and found that 3 percent reported having intentionally used P.G.D. "to select an embryo for the presence of a disability [such as deafness or dwarfism]."

In other words, some [deaf or dwarf] parents had the painful and expensive fertility procedure for the express purpose of having children with a defective gene. It turns out that some mothers and fathers don't view certain genetic conditions as disabilities but as a way to enter into a rich, shared culture. . . .

[Some fear] P.G.D. could be used willy-nilly to make genetic freaks. Yet the same fears pervaded the issue of in vitro fertilization decades ago. The small number of P.G.D. centers selecting for mutations doesn't bother me greatly. After all, even natural reproduction is an error-prone process, since almost 1 percent of all pregnancies are complicated by birth defects—often by more disabling conditions than dwarfism or deafness.

More important, as a physician who helps women dealing with complex fetal diseases, I've learned to respect a family's judgment. Many parents share a touching faith that having children similar to them will strengthen family and social bonds.

Darshak M. Sanghavi, "Wanting Babies Like Themselves, Some Parents Choose Genetic Defects," New York Times, *December 5, 2006.*

choices for their children. We should not discount such fears, but we must keep in mind that conjuring dark scenarios for any potent new technology is easy. . . .

To judge the desirability of trying to forestall any germinal choice technology, we must also determine whether the approach would actually reduce the likelihood of abuse. In the short term, of course, it would. Anything that slows the arrival of a technology delays the day when we have to deal with its consequences. But if advanced germinal technologies will eventually arrive anyway—and even critics generally agree that they will—we must ask which is safer: a path that drives the technologies underground and out of public view, or one that explores them openly; a path that pushes their development into the hands of rogue scientists and states, or one that keeps them in the scientific mainstream; a path with surreptitious funding inspired by visions of black-market profits, or one with aboveboard financing and open-market incentives and constraints.

The answers seem clear. Keeping nascent germinal technology in the open and exploring it in full view lowers rather than raises risks. Openness minimizes surprise developments, warns us of impending social challenges, and allows us to gather information about problems that surface during early implementation. Such cautionary knowledge, which is particularly important with uncertain procedures such as germline manipulation, comes cheaply for society, because while the technology is in its infancy and too expensive and rudimentary to be used much clinically, only small numbers of people are at risk. A critic might argue that even a single damaged child would be too many, but if that well-intentioned idea were to drive policy, we'd have to eliminate cars, ban sports, stop vaccinations, and avoid reproduction altogether.

Given the gruesome experiments conducted in Nazi concentration camps, compulsory sterilization laws in the United States, and the pseudoscience of early eugenics when its philosophy was generally accepted, we are right to worry about tyrannical abuses of germinal choice technologies such as PGD and germline intervention. But tyrants can draw on far simpler technologies to abuse their populations and consolidate their power. Guns, jails, and torture chambers do their work well. Even if we consider only biotechnology, selection and manipulation of human embryos is not the biggest threat of totalitarian regimes. We have much more to fear from the weaponization of smallpox, bubonic plague, or other ancient foes that once infected and killed millions. Advances in medicine and public health had nearly vanquished many of these, but if some nation or terrorist group uses these natural enemies of human life, strengthening and spreading the deadly agents, the consequences could be catastrophic. The anthrax attacks in the aftermath of the World Trade Center disaster of September 2001 have given us a warning.

With reproductive technology, at least we are safe from abuses as long as we preserve our own institutions and freedoms. With freely chosen technologies, our only immediate dangers will be of our own making. The mistakes or malign intentions of others will have little direct impact on us. . . .

Challenging Social Objections

The final assertion is that the ultimate consequences of manipulating our genes will be too dire because obscure and distant dangers lurk behind the revolutionary technologies. Without question, the personal, social, political, and philosophical consequences of human control over our biological destiny are enormous, and no one can know where this path will eventually take us. But we must decide whether this implies that we should try to stop this technology or even slow it down. . . .

The challenges accompanying genetic testing will spill over into the reproductive arena as PGD evolves and the birth of a child with serious genetic infirmities or vulnerabilities becomes avoidable. One of the more troubling arguments against letting parents choose the genes of their future children is that such control would so diminish the numbers of children with genetic diseases that society would begin to ignore those still afflicted. This concern is easy to understand, but by its logic, we should stop medical treatment of ill adults as well. After all, if cured, they might be less committed advocates for others with their condition. But I suspect that this fear is exaggerated. We have limited resources, so reducing the number of people with diseases and disabilities might bring those remaining more, not less, help. Rarer diseases do tend to receive less research funding, but overall, this makes good sense. Progress on common diseases helps more people and frequently speeds the development of treatments for less prevalent disorders. If we first tackle common, tractable illnesses, we can later apply what we learn to rare and resistant ones.

Some bioethicists assert that germinal choice will corrupt the attitudes of parents toward their children and affect children's self-images. But these are merely conjectures. Some parents will obviously be disappointed if their "designer" kids don't turn out as hoped, but no one can say how common such disappointment would be, whether it would persist, or if it would be as prevalent as that which already occurs today. People have children for many reasons and start out with a variety of expectations. Some fathers and mothers are happy no matter what their kids do; others doggedly push them toward predetermined goals. Mate selection is a potent force in shaping our offspring, and we devote much attention to this choice. When we can do even more to influence our children's genetics, we will struggle with these decisions too. Future sources of parental dissatisfaction are easy to predict. Some parents will forgo germinal choice technology and end up wishing they had used it. Others will use it and be disappointed in the results. . . .

A friend of mine who was adopted at an early age said she was happy when her adoptive parents told her as a little girl that they had specially chosen her from all the babies they looked at. To learn that her parents had instead flipped a coin would have been no gift. Perhaps future "designer children" will feel like winners from birth, because they will not have that suspicion that might lurk at the back of our minds when we think of germinal choice. Each of us knows that had embryo screening been in use at the time of our conception, our parents might have chosen another, "better" embryo in our place. . . .

We also have to wonder about the spiritual consequences if we modify our biology. Perhaps an extended human lifespan would change the rhythms of our lives or shift our values in undesirable ways. Genetic selection might leave us purposeless and adrift or entice us to seek what we perceive as human "perfection." Maybe the hubris behind these interventions would somehow corrupt our spirit. Such vexing notions, however, could apply equally well to artificial intelligence, nanotechnology, and other developments now surging forward. Whether or not we alter our biology, our world will change dramatically over the next century. These changes will deeply challenge our values and beliefs. They will bring us losses as well as gains.

The possibility of spiritual decay has been raised many times in many eras. The industrial revolution, global warfare, labor unions, income taxes, universal education, contraception, television, the computer, women's rights, all have brought dramatic shifts in the way we see ourselves. All threatened the status quo. Our world is far from perfect, but if we each could somehow choose to leave the present behind and return to a past era stripped of the romanticism time brings, few of us would go, and I suspect that most who did go would come to regret their choice. . . .

Challenging the "Slippery Slope" Argument

"Slippery slope" is an umbrella term for all our general concerns about coming reproductive technologies. Some bioethicists have argued that once we start down the path of human biological manipulation and germinal choice, we will be unable to turn back. The first steps may seem reasonable, even beneficial, they say, albeit often rhetorically, but one thing will lead to another, and soon we will be changing our genetics in ways we would never have dreamed of. The only protection against the most egregious of imagined possibilities is to draw a line right at the outset and not cross it. [Columnist] George Will asserted just this in an opinion piece: "Positive eugenics, any tailoring of an individual's genetic endowment ...," he wrote, "will put us on a slippery slope to the abolition of man."

The challenge in refuting this argument is that it is so, well, slippery. It requires no evidence of immediate danger and is not weakened by refutations of any specific hypothetical threat. Conjuring up grim futures is easy, and the metaphor of the slippery slope has been used time and again to oppose all kinds of innovations. But if biological manipulation is indeed a slippery slope, then we are already sliding down that slope now and may as well enjoy the ride. After all, we already use birth control, *in vitro* fertilization, and preimplantation genetic diagnosis. We already clone sheep, manipulate mouse genetics, and alter human genes to fight disease.

If we can make choices about technology today [as of 2002], and I believe we can, we will be able to do so in the future. Technology doesn't emerge magically; it depends on the existence of large numbers of people who want it. Today we are actively choosing the technologies that serve us, and if future generations do the same, people's biggest fears will not come to pass.

Periodical Bibliography

The following articles have been selected to supplement the diverse views presented in this chapter.

Charlotte Abott   "Everything Conceivable: How Assisted Reproduction Is Changing Men, Women, and the World," *Advocate*, April 24, 2007.

The Economist   "Wise or Foolish Virgins? Asexual Reproduction," July 28, 2007.

Farmers Guardian   "Cloned Animals on Menu in Next Few Years?" July 13, 2007.

Alison George   "Birth of a New Era," *New Scientist*, June 16, 2007.

Viv Groskop   "The Real Causes of Infertility," *New Statesman*, July 9, 2007.

Fiona MacCallum   "Parenting and Child Development in Families with a Child Conceived through Embryo Donation," *Journal of Psychosomatic Obstetrics & Gynecology*, September 2007.

Peggy Orenstein   "Your Gamete, Myself," *New York Times Magazine*, July 15, 2007.

Sarmishta Subramanian   "Wombs for Rent," *Maclean's*, July 2, 2007.

Alexandra Shimo   "Turning Back the Biological Clock," *Maclean's*, June 11, 2007.

Alastair G. Sutcliffe   "Outcome of Assisted Reproduction," *Lancet*, July 28, 2007.

Fusun Terzioglu   "Anxiety of Infertile Men who Undergo Genetic Testing for Assisted Reproductive Treatment," *Journal of Psychosomatic Obstetrics & Gynecology*, September 2007.

OPPOSING VIEWPOINTS® SERIES

CHAPTER 3

What Ethics Should Guide Organ Transplantation?

Chapter Preface

In 2004, thirty-two-year-old Rob Smitty of Chattanooga, Tennessee, decided he wanted to do "something big" to add meaning to his life. That year he signed on to the Web site MatchingDonors.com and arranged to give one of his kidneys to a total stranger, fifty-eight-year-old Bob Hickey of Eagle, Colorado. The first Internet-arranged organ donation caused an uproar in the field of medicine and in the media. Many discussions ensued about whether matching organ donors with recipients over the Internet is ethical.

Medical doctor Jeremiah Lowney and his patient, Paul Dooley, created MatchingDonors.com in 2004. The idea for the Web site came after Dooley watched his father die from cancer while waiting for a kidney donation to become available. In a conversation with Lowney about the experience, Dooley mentioned that he administered a Web site that matched employees with potential employers. He asked Lowney whether a similar Web site could be developed to match those who needed an organ with potential donors. While researching the idea, Dooley and Lowney came across a National Kidney Foundation survey that asked one thousand respondents whether they would consider live organ donation to a complete stranger. When the two men learned that 25 percent of the respondents answered affirmatively, they decided that a donation Web site was worth a try. By 2006, MatchingDonors.com had over 2,400 potential donors registered on their Web site.

When Rob Smitty agreed to give one of his kidneys to Bob Hickey, he traveled to Colorado to begin the surgical process at St. Luke's Medical Center in Denver. The first operation date was cancelled when Hickey's doctor refused to perform the surgery on ethical grounds. Dr. Igal Kam was concerned that because they were strangers, either Smitty or Hickey stood to profit from the transplant, and exchanging money for organ donation is illegal. After the hospital's Clinical Ethics Committee reviewed a release swearing that the only financial arrangement was for Hickey to pay Smitty's travel costs, they allowed the transplant surgery on October 22, 2004.

Even in lieu of the legal release, some still find Internet organ matching to be unethical for several reasons. One problem with communication via the Internet is that potential donors can lie about their physical health. Ill patients desperate for a donor can become vulnerable to scams. Additionally, MatchingDonors.com interferes with the traditional organ donation system administered by the nonprofit organization United Network for Organ Sharing (UNOS). Donors and recipients using MatchingDonors.com are not subject to UNOS's careful system to ensure fair policies and practices for organ transplants. In response to the reservations about Internet organ sharing, Lowney asks, "Is it ethically acceptable to let seventeen people per day die while waiting for an organ transplant while there are potentially thousands of people out there willing to donate?"

| *"Make it legal to buy and sell organs on the open market. At a stroke this could . . . reduce suffering and save lives."*

The Regulated Sale of Organs for Transplant Is Ethical

Mark Cherry

Bioethicist Mark Cherry argues in the following viewpoint that many of the six thousand people who die in the United States every year while waiting for a donor organ could be saved simply by allowing organs to be bought and sold on the open market. According to Cherry, the ethical benefits—the supply of life-saving organs would increase dramatically from both deceased and living donors, many sellers would be lifted from poverty, and reduced waiting time would cut medical costs—outweigh critics' reluctance to put a price tag on human organs. Mark Cherry is associate professor of philosophy at St. Edward's University in Austin, Texas, and the author of Kidney for Sale by Owner: Human Organs, Transplantation, and the Market.

As you read, consider the following questions:

1. How many people were waiting for transplant organs in the United States in 2003, and how many people received an organ that year, according to the author?

Mark Cherry, "Put Donor Organs on the Open Market," *New Scientist*, August 13, 2005, www.newscientist.com. Reproduced by permission.

2. What legal regulations would minimize unethical practices in the buying and selling of organs, in Cherry's opinion?

3. How does Cherry dispute the argument that only rich people would be served by the open-market sale of organs?

Few ordeals could be more distressing than waiting for a replacement kidney, lung or even heart, knowing that your life depends on receiving one. In the US alone, more than 6,000 people die every year while waiting for an organ transplant, and in the UK [in 2004] the figure was over 400. Many others endure great pain and distress, often in hospital on life support, while queuing for available organs. In 2003 in the US, only around 20,000 out of the 83,000 waiting for transplants received them—a tragedy by anyone's standards.

Remedying the Dire Shortage of Organs

What makes this suffering all the more tragic is that much of it could be prevented, and many more lives saved, by changing the way organs are donated. The change is controversial, but it is simple enough: make it legal to buy and sell organs on the open market. At a stroke this could significantly increase the number and quality of available organs, and so reduce suffering and save lives. This, surely, is the bottom line.

How would it help? For a start, it would allow families to sell the organs of a deceased loved one rather than just donate them. The knowledge that their families would benefit could persuade many more people to become organ donors. But it would also open up more intriguing possibilities. For example, some people might consider a contract in which they agreed to give up their usable organs on their death to a particular buyer and have the money paid to their descendants.

Others might wish to sell a redundant internal organ, such as a kidney, while they were still living. This could be seen as

Not Just More Organs but Better Organs

Some of the unnecessarily tragic consequences of preserving the current ban on organ markets include:

- An expansion of time on the waiting list, which effectively excludes the vast majority of patients on dialysis from getting a transplant unless they have a living donor;

- Recipients who are older and sicker when they come up for transplantation, as a consequence of their extended vintage on dialysis;

- Increasing emotional pressure on any available living donor to donate, and the consequent strain on the altruistic features of donor motivation;

- An upsurge in the practice of international organ trafficking—that is, traveling to a developing country for the purpose of purchasing an organ. . . .

Morally, [a regulated market in kidneys from living donors] would ameliorate terrible suffering by dramatically increasing the organ supply. Politically, it would respect the plurality of views in the nation about the meaning of one's own body. And medically, it would mean not only more organs but better organs—healthier and longer lasting, better matched to their respective recipients, and transplanted earlier in the disease process, often before dialysis is even necessary. . . . The comparative advantages of such a market are many and varied, including:

- The opportunity for truly altruistic living donors to donate, largely free of the incessant moral and emotional pressures of the desperation of their designated recipients; . . .

- For the organ vendor, an opportunity to improve the lives of others through an agreed-upon exchange for a consideration that the vendor deems valuable, in a manner that is both as safe as altruistic donation and fully respectful of the vendor's moral agency.

Benjamin Hippen, "The Case for Kidney Markets,"
New Atlantis, no. 14, Fall 2006.

a valuable way of improving their life circumstances; indeed, some might view it as heroic—saving the life of another, at some risk to themselves. Each of these cases is little different to the current system of organ donation apart from the financial compensation that donors and families would receive. And it could go further: you could have a barter market in which people could trade in redundant internal organs—a slice of healthy liver for a healthy kidney, for example.

Maximizing Fairness, Minimizing Ethical Abuse

Many people may consider such proposals morally repugnant, but I believe such feelings are misplaced. Let's look at some specific criticisms. A common challenge is that an open market would exploit the poor; that it would coerce poor people into selling their organs, something that in better circumstances they would not consider. But why would the market necessarily be exploitative? People would be free to negotiate a bargain in which both parties win: on the one side a life is saved, on the other a family is lifted from poverty.

The fear that unscrupulous entrepreneurs would convince people to part with organs for less than the market price is, I believe, also misplaced. Unlike illicit trading, a legally regulated market should not suffer from such behaviour. For example, it should be possible to set minimum legal prices for organs to ensure that sellers are properly compensated. Countries would have to decide how best to regulate the international organ trade, but this shouldn't be a huge challenge since they already regulate international organ donations.

Another reason why a legal trade would discourage unscrupulous practices is that in legitimate markets, kindness and personal recognition are often crucial for business, allowing partners to build up trust. Customer satisfaction and professionalism lead to profits. Transplantation needs skilled services; hospitals, as providers of highly qualified surgical teams, a suitably sterile environment and medical follow-up, have professional incentives to encourage virtuous tendencies in the market. Surgeons would be unlikely to put their reputation at risk by dealing with black-market traders or con-artists.

Critics of organ trading may claim that only the rich would be able to afford organs, and that the poor would have to wait in line for state-funded transplants. But this is unlikely for several reasons. First, since the market would increase the number of organs, making transplantation more readily available, it would reduce queuing time. As it is usually the poor who wait longest for scarce medical resources, it would benefit them most of all. Second, meeting the medical needs of patients who are waiting for transplants is very costly. By reducing waiting times, the market would also very likely save money for public health insurance programmes. Third, even within a market, private individuals could still donate organs for free out of charity to family members or others in need.

It is time to stop the hand-wringing and consider the facts: the current system of organ transplants is not working, and a market for donors and recipients could help save lives and considerably reduce suffering. Proper regulation would be essential to ensure that the system benefited all those in need, regardless of their income, and that it did not exploit the poor. If we fail to take this opportunity, patients will continue to languish on waiting lists until they run out of time.

> *"A gift [of an organ] carries with it the self's presence in a way that a sale and purchase, for example, do not."*

The Sale of Organs for Transplantation Is Unethical

Gilbert Meilaender

In the following viewpoint, ethicist Gilbert Meilaender asserts that selling human organs, even to ease a dire shortage, even when many people will die without transplants, is unethical for two basic reasons. First, he argues, death is not a problem to be solved by any means possible—it is sad but it is the human condition, and not all means of delaying death are ethical. Second, a body may be a collection of separable organs and may even function normally if one is removed, but a person *is dehumanized if the body is viewed this way. In Meilaender's opinion, only by donating an organ as a gift is its connection to the donor maintained, and the person still whole. Gilbert Meilaender holds the Richard and Phyllis Duesenberg Chair in Theological Ethics at Valparaiso University in Indiana. He is a member of the President's Council on Bioethics and the author of* Bioethics: A Primer for Christians.

Gilbert Meilaender, "Gifts of the Body," *New Atlantis*, no. 13, summer 2006, pp. 25–35.

As you read, consider the following questions:

1. What ethical similarities does Meilaender see in going to any length to procure organs and going to any length to ease a gasoline shortage?

2. What justifiable reason does Meilaender see in people's reluctance to donate their organs?

3. According to the author, how is receiving a gift fundamentally different from buying the same item?

We have trained ourselves to think that organs are the sort of thing that can be *given* in the good cause of saving lives. But it now turns out that there are still more lives to be saved. Why then, exactly, are organs not the sort of thing that can also be sold in this same good cause? If we've learned to think of the organ as a separable part that can be offered to another, if we no longer see this offer as a kind of problematic self-mutilation, then it is hard to know why sale of these separable parts should be forbidden. The organs procured will save more lives and mitigate the shortage that operates as a given in the argument. What more need be said?

[But] in what sense is there a shortage of organs for transplant which *must* be overcome? On what basis, if any, should we suppose that the organs of one's body ought to be available for transplant into the body of another? Without making at least some progress in addressing these questions, I do not know how to think about whether proposals for increasing the number of organs for transplant—in particular, proposals for some sort of market in organs—make moral sense.

Death Is Not a Problem to Be Solved

If a man is dying of kidney failure, and if his life might be prolonged by a transplanted kidney but none is available for him, those connected to him by special bonds of love or loyalty may quite naturally and appropriately feel grief, frustration, even outrage. We are heirs of a tradition of thought that teaches us to honor each person's life as unique and irreplaceable (even though we may not be able really to make sense of this inherited belief apart from reference to the God-relation, which is uniquely individuating for each of us). Although the sympathy any of us feels is inevitably proportioned to the closeness of our bond with one who dies, we are right to honor the grief, frustration, and outrage of those who experience a loved one's death as uniquely powerful.

These quite natural feelings fuel the belief, widely shared in our society, that it is imperative to make more organs available for transplant; however, the same feelings of urgency and desperation also make it difficult to think critically about assumptions driving the transplant system in general. To take a very different example, we may also be experiencing a "shortage" of gasoline in this country. Relative to the demand, the supply is scarcer than we would like. In the face of such a shortage, we could permit drilling in heretofore protected lands or we could ease the general demand for oil by developing alternative energy sources such as nuclear power. We could also learn to moderate our desires and demands for gasoline, altering the pattern of our lives. So there are ways to deal with the gasoline shortage that might work but would—at least in the eyes of some—exact too high a moral price. And there are ways to deal with the shortage that would teach us to modify our desires in such a way that we no longer think in terms of a shortage, but they would entail accepting certain limits on how we live. Upon reflection, we may well decide that neither of these answers to the gasoline shortage is a wise direction to take, but it would be a frivolous person who continued to speak of a "shortage" without considering carefully both sorts of alternatives: exploring new sources of energy, or moderating our demands and expectations. Most of the time, though, when the subject is organ transplantation, we attend only to the search for new ways to procure organs. . . .

The Hidden Costs of Selling Your Kidney

The removal of the kidney would leave an indelible mark in the form of a scar. Were the procedure done laparoscopically, it would be small and not easily distinguished from other surgical interventions. Still, it would be visible, if not to strangers then to intimates. Evidence of the sale would thus be written on the body and speak to moral character. It would point not to heroism and generosity of spirit (intrinsic reward) but to desperation and avariciousness (extrinsic reward). In fact, a study conducted in Iran found that kidney sellers suffered extreme shame in their community. In the United States, the opprobrium might be even greater. Historians of punishment, for example, have proposed that the practice of public torture was abandoned in the 18th century not because the punishments were ineffective, but because citizens shared new and acute sensibilities about bodily integrity, which the spectacle of dismemberment violated. Although a surgical scar does not rise to this level, it may still be asked whether we are ready to countenance the signs of kidney sale.

The everyday consequences of an organ market might create other problems. If kidney sale brought a payment of $125,000 tax free, it would make financial sense to undergo the procedure sooner rather than later. For someone at age 21, investing $125,000, perhaps in a mutual fund, would likely double the sum by age 30. Should one then boast of the sale to a prospective partner? At what point in a relationship would one relate the fact? Would it be presented as having the means for a down payment on a starter home? Would the partner be obliged to sell a kidney in the future to enable a move to a still larger home? Should one anticipate inquiries from prospective in-laws on whether you have yet sold your kidney? Should one anticipate such questions from bill collectors (in India this is not hypothetical), or from welfare or unemployment officers or from attorneys in bankruptcy proceedings? Should one also anticipate parents asking an 18-year-old to sell a kidney to offset substantial college tuition costs, or later, wedding costs?

S.M. Rothman and D.J. Rothman, "The Hidden Cost of Organ Sale,"
American Journal of Transplantation, *February 13, 2006.*

If, however, we were to moderate the demands we make on medicine, we might be less pressured to think in terms of an organ shortage. Alongside our natural desperation at the impending death of one who cannot be replaced, alongside our natural tendency to see death as an evil to be combated, we must set another angle of vision about what it means to be human. Each of us is unique and irreplaceable; that is true. But each of us also shares in the limits of our finite condition; we are mortals. "The receiving of an organ does not," as William F. May once put it, "rescue the living from the need to die. It only defers the day when they will have to do their own dying.". . .

From one angle, as long as one irreplaceable person dies whose life might have been prolonged through transplantation, there will always be an organ shortage. From another angle, that is just the truth of the human condition. If we turn organ procurement into a crusade, we make of death simply a problem to be solved rather than an event to be endured as best we can, with whatever resources of mind and spirit are available to us. To be sure, when a particular person . . . faces death, we confront a problem that calls for our attention and our attempts to cure. But not only that. We also face the human condition that calls for wisdom and care. Sometimes, at least, we will undermine the needed wisdom and care if we think of this person's death as only or primarily a problem which it is imperative that we solve.

The Body Is Not a Collection of Separable Parts

Freed of the sense that we are under some imperative to secure more organs, we may be able to think again of the price we would pay—perhaps, to be sure, a justified price—to increase the supply of organs for transplant. It may be that the limited supply of organs is due to thoughtlessness, selfishness, fear, or simply limited altruism. But it may also be based on weighty—if difficult to articulate—beliefs about the meaning of human bodily life. If our problem is thoughtlessness, selfishness, fear, or limited altruism, financial incentives might "solve" the problem. But if there are deeper reasons at work, reasons that have to do with what we may even call the sacredness of human life in the body, we pay a considerable price if we seize upon certain means to increase the supply of organs for transplant.

Perhaps, then, we should start with the disquieting possibility we might prefer to pass by. Forget the issue that arises farther along the way, whether some kind of market in bodily organs could be morally acceptable. Start farther back with the now widely shared presumption that it is morally acceptable—indeed, praiseworthy—freely to give an organ when this donation may be lifesaving. . . .

Consider the truly living donor—not one in the liminal state of the brain-dead-but-heart-beating cadaver, but one who accepts injury to his or her body in order to relieve the suffering or preserve the life of another (usually, though not always, another to whom one is closely bound by ties of kinship or affection). Transplantation in these circumstances raises profound questions about the relation of organ(s), body, and person.

We need not question the charitable motives of the donor, even what Pope John Paul II termed the "heroism" of such an act. Nonetheless, it involves intending one's own bodily harm in order to do good for another. It is . . . the sort of thing a surgeon would normally not even consider doing. . . . What, then, if anything, makes surgical mutilation acceptable—even good—in the context of transplantation?

One way to address this question would involve trying to overcome the close connection of organ, body, and person. We could train ourselves to think of the organ as entirely separable from the body, and the body as little more than a useful conveyance for the person. Thus, for example, Sally

Satel has recently suggested that thinking of the body's parts as not for sale is "outdated thinking." But, partly because it is not easy so to train ourselves to think otherwise, and partly because the very difficulty of doing so suggests that there might be something dehumanizing about the attempt, we have turned in a quite different direction: the idea of donation. To think of the transplanted organ as a gift means that its connection to the donor's body remains and is recognized. Whatever psychological complications this may entail, it protects us against supposing that our bodies are simply collections of parts that could be "alienated" from ourselves in the way a thing or a commodity can be.

Only a Gift Keeps a Donor a Person, Not a Commodity

One who agrees to donate an organ gives himself or herself—not a thing that is owned, but one's very person. A gift—even a gift of something other than one's body—carries with it the self's presence in a way that a sale and purchase, for example, do not. This accounts, in fact, for the very strange mixture of freedom and obligation that is part of the experience of receiving a gift. One who gives has no obligation to do so and acts, therefore, with a freedom and spontaneity that are not possible for the one who receives that gift. And to receive it is to incur an obligation to use the gift with gratitude. If, to borrow an example from Paul Camenisch, I buy from a retiring professor a rare edition of Kant's works, I have not failed in any obligation of gratitude to him if a year later I give those works to a paper recycling drive. But if, having invested himself in those writings over the years, he now makes a gift of them to me, I am constrained to receive and use the gift with gratitude; for it carries his presence in a way that a purchased commodity could not. . . .

Why such limits to the "gift of life"? The only answer, I think, is that, even when we override it for very important reasons, bodily integrity continues to be a great good that cannot simply be ignored in our deliberations. It continues to exert moral pressure, and, if it permits some gifts of the body, it does not permit any and all. And it exerts this pressure because the person (though more than just body) is present in and through the body—not as a mechanism composed of separable and readily alienable parts, but as a unified living whole that is more, much more, than simply the sum of those parts.

Unless we appreciate the deep-seated and legitimate reasons for hesitation about organ transplantation, we are likely to plunge ahead as if the weightiest imperative under which we labor were fashioning means to procure more organs. If, then, in order to try to solve a perceived shortage of organs, we turn to means of procurement that invite and encourage us to think of ourselves as spiritual overlords, free to use the body and its parts as we see fit in the service of good causes, we may save some lives, but we will begin to lose the meaning of the distinctively human lives we want to save. Even a practice of donating organs can be abused, of course. But permitting organ procurement only through the practice of donation allows us, even if just barely, to retain a sense of connection between the part and the whole, the person and the body— allows us, that is, not to destroy ourselves in seeking to do good.

"The [UNOS organ allocation] policy must engender confidence in the general public that the policy is fundamentally fair."

The Current System of Allocating Organs Is Fair and Ethical

United Network for Organ Sharing

The United Network for Organ Sharing (UNOS) is a nonprofit scientific and education organization that administers the nation's Organ Procurement and Transplantation Network, established by Congress in 1984 to collect data on the patient waiting list and match donated organs to waiting patients. All the nation's organ transplant programs, procurement organizations, and tissue-typing labs are currently linked through UNOS. In the following viewpoint, UNOS defends the network's rationale for allocating organs fairly and ethically, which requires balancing sometimes conflicting goals. For example, minimizing deaths of people on the waiting list is best achieved by transplanting the critically ill, who are most likely to die if they do not receive an organ, but maximizing patient survival is best achieved by transplanting patients before they are critically ill.

United Network for Organ Sharing, "UNOS Rationale for Objectives of Equitable Organ Allocation," *UNOS: Bioethics White Paper*, www.unos.org. Reproduced by permission.

As you read, consider the following questions:

1. What percentage of kidney transplants that are a perfect tissue match are still functioning two years later, as reported by UNOS? What percentage of kidneys that are poorly matched are still functioning?

2. According to UNOS, why do nonwhite patients wait significantly longer than whites for transplant organs?

3. How does the geographical allocation of hearts and lungs differ from the geographical allocation of other organs, as explained by UNOS?

Organ donation, procurement, distribution and allocation are all intrinsically linked together. Thus, organ allocation cannot be addressed in a vacuum without considering the impact of any allocation policy on the supply of transplantable organs. The policy should strive to avoid loss of organs, and it should also promote recovery of the most organs possible. The policy must engender confidence in the general public that the policy is fundamentally fair to accomplish these two purposes. It must promote efficient organ recovery at the same time. Organs have severely limited timeframes in which they remain useable for transplants. Therefore, the policy must also promote efficient organ distribution to avoid organs becoming less beneficial or wasted because they were not transplanted soon enough.

Maximize Patient and Graft Survival

The way in which donor organs are matched with waiting recipients may affect the survival of the transplant itself (graft survival) and the survival of the patient. Many medical factors determine whether a transplant is medically feasible at all and whether the chances of long-term success are as high as possible. The allocation policy should not result in an organ being offered to a transplant center for a particular patient if the transplant is not medically feasible (e.g., positive crossmatch, inappropriate organ size or incompatible blood type).

The degree of medical compatibility between the donor and candidate may also affect the long-term survival. For example, it is widely accepted that transplanting a kidney with tissue antigens that perfectly match those of the recipient stands a better chance of long-term success than transplanting a kidney from a donor whose antigens do not match. Two years after a transplant, 86% of patients who receive a perfect "6 antigen match" have a functioning kidney. In contrast, only 72% of patients who receive a poorly matched kidney have a functioning graft two years after transplant.

The Waiting List patient's medical condition may also influence whether the transplant will be successful. For example, 51% of patients who receive a liver transplant when they are gravely ill (hospitalized in the intensive care unit just prior to transplant) survive at least two years. In contrast, 77–80% of liver Waiting List patients who receive transplants before they are sick enough to be continuously hospitalized survive at least two years. Slightly more than 10% of patients who receive a liver transplant when they are in the most urgent status are retransplanted as compared to 6 to 8% in the less urgent categories. . . .

It is important for all transplant candidates as a group that the allocation policy try to achieve the best transplant survival rates possible. This reduces the number of organs needed for patients whose grafts fail. Every repeat transplant denies someone else either a life-saving opportunity or a chance at a better quality of life because there are not enough organs available for everyone who needs a transplant. A policy that results in low overall survival by transplanting patients whose condition has worsened to the point that their chances of survival have diminished will perpetuate the likelihood that patients who are not as sick and have a higher probability of a successful transplant will be forced to wait until their condition worsens and their chances for success are also diminished.

Minimize Disparities in Waiting Times and Deaths While Waiting

The policy should be designed to treat people in similar situations as much the same as possible, in order to promote overall equity. It is unreasonable to expect that every patient will have the same opportunity to receive a transplant, because circumstances are different for individual patients and for certain groups of patients with special conditions. For example, patients with panel reactive antibody (PRA) levels of 99 (meaning that the patient's immune system will reject kidneys from approximately 99% of all donors) will not have the same opportunities to receive kidney transplants as patients with PRAs of zero. . . .

The policy should provide a degree of priority to patients who need transplants most urgently to minimize the number of Waiting List deaths. Critically ill patients are the ones most likely to die waiting for a transplant. . . .

Maximize Opportunity for Patients with Biological or Medical Disadvantages

Allocation policy should make it possible for patients with certain medical or biological disadvantages to receive optimal opportunities for transplants. Some patients have biological or medical conditions that make it more difficult for them to receive a transplant. The allocation policy must sometimes give these patients additional consideration in order for them to receive an equitable opportunity. For example, it is very difficult to find compatible kidneys for patients with high levels of antibodies against foreign tissue antigens known as human leukocyte antigens (HLA). Such patients are said to be highly sensitized. Patients can develop antibodies to HLA after blood

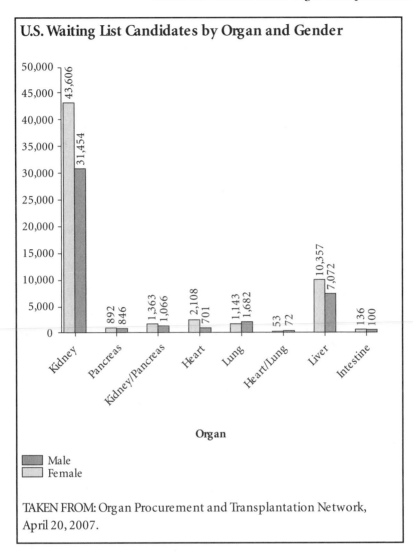

U.S. Waiting List Candidates by Organ and Gender

50,000
45,000
40,000
35,000
30,000
25,000
20,000
15,000
10,000
5,000
0

Kidney — 43,606 / 31,454
Pancreas — 892 / 846
Kidney/Pancreas — 1,363 / 1,066
Heart — 2,108 / 701
Lung — 1,143 / 1,682
Heart/Lung — 53 / 72
Liver — 10,357 / 7,072
Intestine — 136 / 100

Organ

■ Male
□ Female

TAKEN FROM: Organ Procurement and Transplantation Network, April 20, 2007.

transfusions, pregnancies, or previous transplants. Highly sensitized patients would rarely be offered a suitable kidney if the policy did not give them extra consideration. . . .

Children are medically disadvantaged, because they do not grow and develop well without normal kidney function. The longer they wait for kidneys, the more their growth is permanently stunted. Therefore, it seems fair to give children extra consideration in the kidney allocation policy. . . .

A person's race *per se* is not a factor in the present allocation system. However, it has become clear in the U.S., where the organ donor and organ recipient populations are predominantly white, that Waiting List patients of other races have significantly longer average waiting times before being transplanted than do whites. There may be many confounding variables affecting these differences. Several biological factors are known to contribute to the problem. For example, certain blood types (types O and B) are more common among blacks than among whites. Blacks represent 12% of the general population and donate 12% of the kidneys that are transplanted. However, 32% of patients awaiting a kidney transplant are black because there is a higher incidence of end stage renal disease among blacks. It is more difficult to provide kidney transplants for black patients with type O or B blood because more than 80% of kidney donors are white and 12% are black. . . .

Minimize Effects Related to Geography

Ideally, allocation policy should not disadvantage certain patients because of the part of the country in which they live. However, the availability of deceased donor organs can vary widely from one area to another for many reasons. It is not currently feasible to distribute organs using a single national Waiting List because they can last only a limited time without oxygenated blood and for other technical reasons (e.g., the necessity of crossmatching before kidney transplants). Doing so might distribute organs more equally across the nation, but it would result in unacceptable organ damage and wasted organs. For this reason, organs are currently distributed to patient populations that are smaller than the entire national population but are not so large that transporting organs from donor to patient will result in unacceptable ischemia time (time without oxygenated blood). . . .

The current system attempts to reduce geographical differences in organ distribution. The OPTN [Organ Procurement and Transplantation Network] keeps records on every patient in the U.S. waiting for a deceased donor organ transplant. As each organ becomes available, it is generally allocated first using a list of patients known as the local list. That list includes patients who are registered for transplants at specific transplant centers within the service area where the donor is located. If the organ is not suitable for a patient on the local list, a larger list is used, which for organs other than hearts and lungs, includes all patients listed in the same UNOS geographic region as the donor. For hearts, concentric circles of 500 mile radii from the site of the donor are used. The national list is used for organs other than hearts and lungs only if there is no suitable local or regional patient. An exception to this process exists in the kidney allocation system, according to which, each kidney is compared first with the composite national list, in an effort to identify all patients whose HLA identically match those of the donor. . . .

Allow Convenient Access to Transplantation

Allowing convenient access to transplantation for patients relates to the principle of striving to give equal consideration to medical utility and justice. A primary concern to many patients who require transplantation is that they be able to receive medical treatment without the burden of traveling great distances. The seriousness of their illness for some patients will also affect their ability to travel great distances in order to receive a transplanted organ. Local hospitalization may also be important so that transplant recipients can receive visits from close family members and maintain their morale during recovery. Therefore, geographic and logistical concerns should be considered in the organ allocation system so that patients who cannot medically, physically, or financially afford to travel great distances to receive a transplant are not disadvantaged

| "Changing the national organ allocation system could save thousands of lives a year and improve the system's fairness."

The Current System of Allocating Organs Is Unfair and Unethical

David J. Undis

In the following viewpoint, David J. Undis argues that the current system of organ allocation is unethical because it gives organs to patients who will not donate their own organs when there are registered organ donors who need that organ—in Undis's view, "awarding the lottery jackpot to someone who did not buy a ticket." He contends that allocating organs first to registered organ donors is an ethical solution that will lead millions of people to register, solve the organ shortage, and save thousands of lives every year. David J. Undis is the executive director of LifeSharers, a nonprofit voluntary network of organ donors, based in Nashville, Tennessee, whose members give fellow members preferred access to their organs.

David J. Undis, "Changing Organ Allocation Will Increase Organ Supply," *DePaul Law Review*, vol. 55, April 26, 2006, pp. 889–896. Reproduced by permission.

As you read, consider the following questions:

1. How many Americans died waiting for organs in 2004, and how many are on the national waiting list as of 2006, according to the author?

2. What percentage of Americans are currently signed up to donate their organs when they die, according to Undis?

3. In Undis's opinion, how can UNOS give transplant priority to registered organ donors without seeking congressional approval?

Imagine that the United Network for Organ Sharing (UNOS) made the following announcement tomorrow: "Beginning January 1 of next year, we will make no human organ available for transplantation into any person who is not a registered organ donor. The only exceptions will be directed donations and cases where no registered organ donor matches an organ that is available." Following the announcement of this policy change, millions and millions of people would register themselves and their children as organ donors. Wouldn't you, too?

Twenty Thousand More Organs Per Year

Registering as an organ donor would give you a better chance of getting an organ if you ever needed one. Deciding not to register would reduce your chance. When you consider that more than half of the people on transplant waiting lists in the United States will die before they get a transplant, improving your odds could literally mean the difference between life and death. Agreeing to donate your organs after you die is a small price to pay for a better chance to get an organ if you ever need one to live. Almost everyone would decide to pay that price. The supply of organs would increase, and thousands of lives would be saved every year.

In 2004, about 7,000 deceased organ donors in the United States provided the organs for about 20,000 transplants. But organs are transplanted from less than half of the eligible deceased donors. That means we could obtain 20,000 additional organs every year by changing the organ allocation system. To put that number in perspective, keep in mind that in 2004, 7,305 people were removed from the national transplant waiting list because they died, and 1,663 more were removed because they became too sick to undergo surgery. With an additional 20,000 organs per year, we could eliminate most of those deaths, reduce the size of the waiting list, and shorten waiting times for people still on the list.

We do not need medical breakthroughs to achieve these results. All we need is behavior change. Only about forty percent of Americans have signed up to donate their organs when they die. And Americans donate less than half of the organs that could be transplanted. The rest are buried or cremated. All we need to do is convince people to stop throwing away organs that could save their neighbors' lives. Changing how we allocate organs will produce that behavior change.

The idea of giving registered organ donors an allocation preference is not new. It has been around for more than fifteen years. Everyone who has suggested this idea has predicted that it would significantly increase the supply of organs: Some have said it would completely eliminate the waiting list.

A Simple Matter of Justice

But is it fair to allocate organs first to registered organ donors? Yes, in fact it makes the organ allocation system fairer. What is not fair is giving an organ to someone who will not donate his or her own, when there is a registered organ donor who needs it. It is like awarding the lottery jackpot to someone who did not buy a ticket.

Serving registered organ donors first is a simple matter of justice. Justice demands that people who are the same should

America Needs an Opt-Out, Not Opt-In, Organ Donor System

[The] unfortunate wait for organs occurs by virtue of an insufficient system of donation known as an opt-in system. To be an organ donor, you must fill out the proper forms and opt to participate in the organ donor registry run by the United Network for Organ Sharing. According to this group, there were 5,000 living donors in 2005. That year, almost 30,000 patients were removed from the organ waiting list, thanks to such donors. Sounds successful, right? Unfortunately, 15% removed from the list—four-and-a-half thousand patients—died still waiting for their organs. And every year the wait lengthens; though so many were removed from the list, it actually grew by 4,000 in 2005. . . .

This terribly long waiting list is caused by numerous problems, some of which are sorer losses than others. For one, families have the legal right not to donate their loved one's body, even if the person had explicitly asked to be a donor in his will. . . .

We must recognize these impediments, and use law to erase them. Therefore I propose that there be no familial overrides if the deceased person's will was clearly stated before death. And, more importantly, that we emulate Europe's opt-out organ donation system in which everyone is by default a donor unless they complete the forms to opt out of the donor registry. Anytime an adult checks into a hospital he could be presented the forms, and [unless he knowingly opts out], if he dies in a hospital his organs may be transplanted for health purposes.

Such is the way of multiple European countries—Spain, France, Sweden, Greece, Hungary, even Belgium has recognized the advantages, and this system aught be embraced by us as well. Organs aren't reaped from anyone and everyone that dies, but rather, only if a particular organ matches a person within the area. Perhaps it seems a violation of rights, but remember, the decision to donate or not remains with the individual. Opting out is always an option to everyone.

Nihar Patel, "Organ Donation,"
Thrive Wire Health Media, *July 26, 2006.*

be treated the same. But the person who has not agreed to donate his or her organs when he or she dies is not the same as the person who has. There is an ethically relevant difference between the two.

Imagine that a heart is available for transplant. Imagine also that two people are a good match for the heart: Mr. Donor, who has committed to donate his organs when he dies, and Mr. Keeper, who has not. Given the shortage of organs, and given that Mr. Keeper's only alternatives to donating his organs are to bury them or burn them, should we treat Mr. Donor and Mr. Keeper as if there is no ethically relevant difference between them? No, Mr. Keeper's failure to donate his organs is a spectacularly selfish act. He would throw away his organs instead of saving the lives of his neighbors—and those are his only available choices. It boggles the mind to suggest that his claim to an organ is ethically the same as Mr. Donor's. Mr. Donor should get that heart, even if Mr. Keeper is sicker or has been waiting longer. Mr. Keeper has no moral claim to an organ. Giving the heart to Mr. Donor serves the cause of justice.

Perhaps more importantly, rewarding Mr. Donor's decision to donate his organs encourages others to do the same. This encouragement saves lives. On the other hand, giving that heart to Mr. Keeper encourages others to delay signing donor cards or to refuse to sign them, and that encouragement lets more people on the transplant waiting list suffer and die.

Giving organs first to organ donors encourages people to donate their organs. Giving them to nondonors does not.

But under UNOS's allocation rules, most organs are given to nondonors. In fact, UNOS allocates about sixty percent of all organs to people who have not agreed to donate their own organs when they die. As long as we allow people who refuse to donate to jump to the front of the waiting list if they need a transplant, we will always have an organ shortage.

Without organ donors there can be no organ transplants. Giving organs first to organ donors produces more organ donors, and that saves more lives. The primary goal of the organ allocation system should be to save as many lives as possible. Other goals should be secondary.

UNOS Does Not Need Congressional Approval to Make This Change

It would be simple for UNOS to change its allocation system to put registered organ donors first. UNOS could simply add a field to its waiting list database which would show whether a potential organ recipient is a registered organ donor. Then when an organ becomes available, instead of offering it first to the highest-ranked person on its match run, UNOS could offer it first to the highest-ranked registered donor.

Putting organ donors first has an important advantage over most other suggestions for increasing the supply of organs. No legislative action is needed to implement it. UNOS already has the authority to give registered organ donors an allocation preference. The UNOS Ethics Committee acknowledged this fact in its 1993 white paper titled "Preferred Status For Organ Donors," in which it wrote: "A trial could be implemented without requiring any alteration in existing legislation. . . ." In fact, UNOS already moves live donors up the waiting list if they later need a transplant. UNOS can, and should, do the same for people who agree to donate when they die.

Congress has never made tackling the organ shortage a priority, and there is no reason to think it will do so in the foreseeable future. Anyone who cares about the more than 90,000 people now on the national transplant waiting list should welcome an approach to increasing the organ supply that does not depend on legislative action.

To review, changing the national organ allocation system could save thousands of lives a year and improve the system's fairness. And UNOS has the power to implement this simple change. So, what is UNOS's position on this? It has not really taken one.

The closest UNOS came to adopting this proposed change was in 1993. But its white paper on the subject ultimately stopped short. It only recommended "wider societal discussion before considering concrete plans for implementation" of any system.

UNOS, however, has not led the discussion it recommended. It has been largely silent on the subject since the publication of its white paper twelve years ago. That is unfortunate because over 55,000 people on the UNOS waiting list have died in the last ten years. Most of those deaths could have been prevented.

> "With over ninety thousand people and rising on the organ waiting list, there is widespread interest in finding novel ways to boost the organ supply."

Novel Ways to Increase the Organ Supply Should Be Considered

Sam Crowe and Eric Cohen

Sam Crowe is a policy analyst with the President's Council on Bioethics, a federal commission created in 2001 by George W. Bush to advise the president on ethical issues related to biomedical science and technological advances. Eric Cohen, a former senior consultant to the council, is editor at large for the New Atlantis *and an adjunct fellow at the Ethics and Public Policy Center in Washington, D.C. In the following viewpoint, Crowe and Cohen present innovative proposals for increasing the supply of transplant organs, the ethics of which council members debated in 2006 and 2007. Whether modest (educating people about the need for donor organs) or radical (harvesting of organs after death even in the absence of consent), Crowe and Cohen argue that all these proposals deserve study in the face of the serious organ shortage.*

Sam Crowe and Eric Cohen, "Organ Transplant Policies and Policy Reforms," *Discussion Aid for the September 2006 President's Council on Bioethics Meeting*, September 2006, www.bioethics.gov.

As you read, consider the following questions:

1. Without directly paying for a transplant organ, what associated costs of donation might government agencies pay for to encourage living donation, according to Crowe and Cohen?

2. What is the UNOS upper age limit for organ donation, according to the authors, and what increased age limit do they suggest?

3. How do the two kinds of organ exchanges—list donation and paired exchanges—differ, as described by Crowe and Cohen?

No matter how one frames the issue, the supply of organs is not meeting the demand. With over ninety thousand people and rising on the organ waiting list, there is widespread interest in finding novel ways to boost the organ supply—ranging from modest reforms of the current system, such as better education about the benefits of organ donation, to more radical proposals, such as organ markets, the redefinition of death, and the retrieval of organs from deceased individuals without their prior consent. . . .

Expand Education Programs

For the past few decades, education and outreach about the benefits of organ donation—the "gift of life," as it is regularly called—have been promoted, supported, or undertaken by the federal government, state governments, and myriad private organizations. These efforts could be significantly expanded. National campaigns might take the form of an "organ donor awareness day," where the President and Congress issue proclamations or commemoratives explaining the need for and virtues of organ donation. Congress might promote an extensive publicity program that targets communities throughout the country that have low donation rates. States might have similar programs, and they might further expand their education efforts at their DMVs, public schools, and driver's education courses. Local communities might also sponsor donor awareness events, such as parades or carnivals. One might even make the education campaign more aggressive—by declaring organ donation a national duty, or shaming those who do not register as organ donors as "wasting the gift of life.". . .

Remove Disincentives for Living Donation

Disincentives are the financial costs a potential organ donor might incur during the process of living donation. Some of the most significant disincentives are: lost pay and forgone advancement due to missed work; the costs of transportation, from the initial visit to determine eligibility for donation to the final trip home after transplantation and recovery; lodging and perhaps food during these trips; and any other financial costs directly related to the donation process.

Already, the federal government and a few states have laws that aim to ease the economic burden of being a living donor. These laws mainly apply to government employees and typically only reduce a portion of the donation costs. A more comprehensive policy would cover most, if not all, of the financial costs incurred during the donation process. . . .

The Use of Expanded-Criteria Donors

One way to expand the potential pool of organ donors is to loosen the health criteria for being a donor at death. Already . . . we use both "standard donors" who meet the strictest standards of eligibility and "expanded criteria donors" who meet a looser, more discretionary standard. The UNOS [United Network for Organ Sharing] Board of Directors defines the eligible dead donor as an individual who is 70 years or younger and meets a very extensive list of health requirements. There are two main ways of expanding this definition. First, the age limit might be increased to 75 or 80. Second, some of the health requirements imposed on potential donors

Finding Organ Donors on the Internet

One of 95,000 people who may have to wait as long as 10 years for a new kidney via the federal government's United Network for Organ Sharing (UNOS) list, [Rahwe] Daniel found a new organ in an unconventional way: She went online. MatchingDonors.com, a two-year-old non-profit Web site, connects those in need of healthy body organs with people ready to donate them. . . .

While at a dialysis session, Daniel noticed an article about MatchingDonors.com, launched in 2004 by Dr. Jeremiah Lowney of New England and Baptist Hospital and Paul Dooley. Site officials say it has successfully brought about 39 live-donor kidney transplants, with another 40 scheduled in 2007. Those seeking organs pay a fee ranging from $49 a week to $595 for unlimited usage, to cover site upkeep and advertising costs. (The charge is waived for those who can't afford it—about 70 percent of the site's members, says Dooley—and Medicare has approved reimbursement to services like MatchingDonors.) Potential donors can surf their Web pages for free.

Marisa Wong, "Kidneys Online,"
People, *March 26, 2007.*

might be reduced. Serious diseases such as AIDS would still disqualify the use of organs, but less severe conditions might not. . . .

The Promotion of Organ Exchanges

One possible way to expand the donor pool is to promote and facilitate organ exchanges. In some cases, an individual wishes to act as a living donor for a loved one, but cannot do so because he or she is not biologically compatible with the intended recipient. An organ exchange would permit the living donor to give his or her organ to someone else in exchange for the intended recipient receiving an organ from another source. There are two main forms of such exchanges: list donations and paired exchanges.

A list donation occurs when Donor A desires to give a kidney to Recipient A, but the two individuals are not biologically compatible. Instead, Donor A gives a kidney to someone on the general kidney list, and in exchange Recipient A receives a compatible kidney from the list. Depending on how such a policy is enacted, Recipient A could receive a certain number [of] points to improve his or her list ranking, meaning he or she would get a kidney earlier but not immediately. Or the intended recipient could be moved up to the top of the list, meaning that he or she would get the next publicly available kidney. . . .

A paired exchange is similar to list donation, but it involves two living donors instead of one living donor and a kidney from the list. In other words: Donor A gives to Intended Recipient B, and Donor B gives to Intended Recipient A. Paired exchanges can also occur among multiple pairs of donors and recipients. For example: the donor from pair A has a kidney that matches the recipient of pair B. The donor of pair B has a kidney that matches the recipient of pair C. And the donor of pair C has a kidney that matches the recipient of pair A. Each donor can then offer a kidney to a compatible recipient, allowing three donations to occur instead of (in some cases) none at all. . . .

Presumed Consent

Presumed consent means that the government assumes that citizens agree to donate their organs at death unless the individual or the family explicitly declares otherwise. Such policies vary based upon *how easy* it is to "opt out" and based on who has the *authority* to opt out: a hard presumed consent law might permit only the individual, before death, to opt out, meaning that surviving family members would have no authority to prevent organ procurement if their deceased loved one had remained silent. A softer presumed consent law might authorize surviving family members to opt out, but only if they take the initiative to intervene; or, such a law could require organ procurement agencies to inform family members that organs are being taken, giving them an explicit opportunity to opt out. . . .

Organ Conscription

An organ conscription policy would mandate that all available organs be removed from the deceased, regardless of the wishes of individuals or families. Such a law is not at present being seriously contemplated in the United States, but it is worth noting here to show what might be embraced by those who take the pursuit of health as their only or most important guide to organ policy. A conscription policy would maximize the number of available organs from deceased donors, and it would eliminate the added complexity of creating donor registries and seeking permission from surviving family members. It would treat organs as a societal resource that the needy have a right to acquire. Just as we might conscript individuals to act as soldiers in wartime, we might conscript the newly dead to act as sources of spare parts in the struggle to save or improve the lives of those suffering from organ failure. It would take something that the dead will never need again to give it to the living who desperately need it. . . .

New Rewards or Incentives for Organ Donation

One range of policy options involves creating new incentives or offering new rewards for being an organ donor. While disincentives are the costs that originate with the act of donation, incentives are the rewards offered to those who donate. These potential incentives vary significantly in type, and include: (1) public honors or medals for organ donors and/or their families; (2) gifts to charity in the name of the donor; (3) preferred status as a potential donor recipient; (4) health insurance coverage for living donors or insurance premium reductions for those who agree to donate their organs after death; (5) life and disability insurance for living donors; (6) payment of a deceased donor's funeral expenses. . . .

[Government policy makers] would do well to keep in mind the human goods at stake in our organ policy—health, freedom, and dignity central among them—as well as the moral and practical arguments for preserving crucial elements of the current system. In an area as complex as organ transplantation, the pursuit of some goods always risks compromising others, and the preservation of even the most important goods may leave us to endure a heavy weight—including the weight of those who suffer and often die waiting for organs that never come.

| "Fears abound that policies to maximize
  organ donations could go too far."

Novel Ways to Increase the Organ Supply Are Ethically Unsound

University of Minnesota's Center for Bioethics

The Center for Bioethics, founded at the University of Minnesota in 1985 and directed by Jeffrey Kahn as of 2007, is a research, education, and advisory group concerned with ethical issues in the biological sciences. In the following viewpoint, the center presents ethical objections to many proposals offered as innovative strategies for increasing the supply of transplant organs from cadaver donors, living donors, and alternative sources. For example, the center argues that offering donors financial incentives coerces people to donate when they really do not want to, and that radical proposals such as harvesting organs from condemned prisoners are morally repugnant.

As you read, consider the following questions:

1. When a mandated choice policy was tested in Texas, how many people chose *not* to donate organs, according to the center?

University of Minnesota's Center for Bioethics, "Ethics of Organ Transplantation," February 2004. Reproduced by permission.

2. What drawbacks of living donation might poor people overlook if they were offered financial incentives to donate their organs, in the authors' view?

3. According to the *JAMA* study cited by the authors, what percentage of people in India who sold their kidneys to pay off debt were still in debt six years later? What percentage reported their health had deteriorated since donation?

One way to avoid the ethical problems associated with the shortage of transplantable organs is to increase the number of donor organs. However, fears abound that policies to maximize organ donations could go too far—leading to organ farming or premature declarations of death in order to harvest organs.

Many, if not most, people agree that taking organs from any source is a justifiable practice within certain ethical boundaries. Controversies result from an inability to define exactly where those boundaries lie. Everyone may have their own unique ideas about the boundaries they would like to see concerning the following three sources of transplantable organs: cadaveric donors, living donors and alternative organ sources. . . .

Concerns About Cadaver Strategies

Since one cadaveric donor can provide multiple organs, this is a natural place to look to increase the number of available organs. Efforts to increase the number of cadaveric donors have met with much debate and controversy.

[One] potential strategy to increase organs from cadaveric donors is mandated choice. Under this strategy, every American would have to indicate their wishes regarding organ transplantation, perhaps on income tax forms or drivers licenses. When a person dies, the hospital must comply with their written wishes regardless of what their family may want. The positive aspect of this strategy is that it strongly enforces the concept of individual autonomy of the organ donor.

A mandated choice policy would require an enormous level of trust in the medical system. People must be able to trust their health care providers to care for them no matter what their organ donation wishes. A 2001 survey of 600 family members who had experience donating organs from a deceased loved one found about 25% of respondents would be concerned that a doctor wouldn't do as much to save their loved one's life if they knew they were willing to donate their organs.

A mandated choice policy was tested in Texas during the 1990s. When forced to choose, almost 80% of the people chose NOT to donate organs, which was not an increase in the number of available organs. The law enacting mandated choice for Texans has since been repealed. . . .

[Another] strategy under consideration to increase cadaveric organ donation is the use of incentives. Incentives take many forms. Some of the most frequently debated incentive strategies are:

1. Give assistance to families of a donor with funeral costs
2. Donate to a charity in the deceased person's name if organs are donated
3. Offer recognition and gratitude incentives like a plaque or memorial
4. Provide financial or payment incentives . . .

Some ethicists believe that many of the in incentives above, while not attached directly to cash money, are still coercive and unfair. They believe that some people will be swayed to donate, in spite of their better judgment, if an incentive is attractive enough. They further argue that a gesture may seem small and a mere token to one person, but others might interpret it quite differently.

Internet Organ-Donation Sites Are Unethical

Organizations like MatchingDonors.com, [says Harvard Medical School professor Douglas Hanto] open the system to abuse. They allow the possibility of payment-for-organ-donations, which is illegal. They bypass a fair waiting system. They don't provide for medical screening that ensures the donated organs are not "wasted" by going to patients who will die from other causes anyway.

Such private donations can also favor people of means because they have the resources to pay the $295 monthly subscription fees charged by MatchingDonors.com and potentially favor people who are physically attractive or whose personal story is particularly poignant.

Alvin Powell, "HMS Examines Ethics of Internet Organ Donation,"
Harvard University Gazette, May 19, 2005.

A final anti-incentives argument offered by some ethicists discourages the practice of incentivizing organ donation. They believe that society should instead re-culture its thinking to embrace a communitarian spirit of giving and altruism where people actively *want* to donate their organs.

Using Organs from Executed Prisoners

[Another] strategy under consideration to increase the number of available cadaveric organs is to use organs taken from prisoners who are put to death. One argument in favor of taking organs from prisoners who are put to death is that it is the execution that is ethically unsound and not the organ removal. Indeed, in light of the severe organ shortage, some ethicists could make the argument that to not use the organs for transplantation is wasteful. John Robertson, in a 1999 article, put forth the argument that obtaining organs from condemned prisoners is allowable if the prisoner or their next of kin consents to donation, as long as organ donation is not the means by which the prisoner is killed because that violates the principle that a cadaveric donor be dead prior to donation. Finally, some could argue that organ retrieval from executed prisoners is morally justifiable only if a "presumed consent" donation practice was in place.

Many, if not most, bioethicists consider taking organs from condemned prisoners a morally objectionable practice. Colorful language used by some ethicists includes the following words to describe the practice: "immoral," "repugnance," and "revulsion." . . .

Concerns About Living Organ Donations

Not everyone encourages the practice of living donation for all people. Drawbacks to becoming a living donor may include:

- Health consequences: Pain, discomfort, infection, bleeding and potential future health complications are all possible
- Psychological consequences: Family pressure, guilt or resentment
- Pressure: Family members may feel pressured to donate when they have a sick family member or loved one
- No donor advocate: While the patients have advocates, like the transplant surgeon or medical team (who are there to advise the patient and work in favor of his or her best interests) donors do not have such an advocate and can be faced with an overwhelming and complicated process with no one to turn to for guidance or advice

A few medical and ethical professionals argue that living donation is inappropriate under any circumstances and should not only be discouraged but abandoned all together because of the risk and dangers associated with donating organs. Other critics seek to discourage living donation because they think extending life through costly and physically taxing medical procedures is not the purpose of health and healthcare in America. . . .

Opposition to Buying and Selling Organs

Financial incentives aimed at encouraging living donation have received much attention from bioethicists lately. Most experts argue that buying and selling human organs is an immoral and disrespectful practice. The moral objection raised most often argues that selling organs will appeal to the socioeconomically disadvantaged (people who are poor, uneducated, live in a depressed area, etc.) and these groups will be unfairly pressured to sell their organs by the promise of money. This pressure could also cause people to overlook the possible drawbacks in favor of cash incentives. On the other hand, wealthy people would have unfair access to organs due to their financial situations.

The current United States policy does not allow for the sale of human organs. The National Organ Transplant Act of 1984 banned such a practice.

In 2002, an article that examined the effects of offering payment for kidneys in India was published in the *Journal of the American Medical Association*. Although critics pointed to a variety of methodological issues, the findings uncovered some interesting data:

- 96% of people sold their kidneys to pay off debt
- 74% of people who sold their kidneys still had debt 6 years later
- 86% of people reported a deterioration in their health status after donation
- 79% would not recommend to others that they sell their kidneys. . .

Objections to Alternative Organ Sources

With the state of discrepancy between organ donors and people waiting for an organ transplant, researchers and advocates have begun to consider non-traditional donation. Some potential non-traditional sources of organs are:

1. *Animal Organs*: Animals are a potential source of donated organs. Experiments with baboon hearts and pig liver transplants have received extensive media attention in the past. One cautionary argument in opposition to the use of animal organs concerns the possibility of transferring animal bacteria and viruses to humans.

2. *Artificial Organs*: Artificial organs are yet another potential option. The ethical issues involved in artificial organs often revert to questions about the cost and effectiveness of artificial organs. People who receive artificial organ transplants might require further transplanting if there is a problem with the device.

3. *Stem Cells*: Stem cells are cells that can specialize into the many different cells found in the human body. Researchers have great hopes that stem cells can one day be used to grow entire organs, or at least groups of specialized cells. The ethical objections concerning stem cells have focused primarily on their source. While stem cells can be found in the adult human body, the seemingly most potent stem cells come from the first few cells of a human embryo. When the stem cells are removed, the embryo is destroyed. Some people find this practice morally objectionable and would like to put a stop to research and medical procedures that destroy human embryos in the process.

4. *Aborted Fetuses*: Aborted fetuses are a proposed source of organs. Debates address whether it is morally appropriate to use organs from a fetus aborted late in a pregnancy for transplantation that could save the life of another infant. Many people believe that this practice would condone late-term abortions, which some individuals and groups find morally objectionable. Another objection comes from people who fear that encouraging the use of aborted fetal organs would encourage "organ farming," or the practice of conceiving a child with the intention of aborting it for its organs.

"Those who do not object to the killing of pigs for [food, insulin, and heart valves] should surely have no objection to killing pigs to provide whole organs."

Animal-to-Human Organ Transplantation Is Ethical

Cindy A. Smetanka and David K.C. Cooper

In the following viewpoint, researchers Cindy A. Smetanka and David K.C. Cooper ethically justify xenotransplantation—animal-to-human transplantation—as a technology with enormous potential to treat disease and save lives. Smetanka and Cooper maintain that the risks of cross-species infection and organ rejection have been significantly reduced and that the most likely animal donors, pigs (which are already killed for food and medical therapies), will be treated extremely humanely. Moreover, they argue, using animal organs resolves some of the ethical objections to human organ transplantation. Smetanka is assistant professor and Cooper is professor of surgery at the Thomas E. Starzl Transplantation Institute of the University of Pittsburgh Medical Center, a leading research and clinical center for patients with end-stage organ failure.

Cindy A. Smetanka and David K.C. Cooper, "The Ethics Debate in Relation to Xenotransplantation," *Scientific and Technical Review*, vol. 24, no. 1, April 2005, pp. 335–342. Reproduced by permission.

As you read, consider the following questions:

1. What ethical objections to *human* organ donation would no longer be an issue if animal organs are used for transplantation, according to the authors?

2. How have scientists reduced the risk of transmitting porcine endogenous retroviruses (PERV) to humans during xenotransplantation, according to Smetanka and Cooper?

3. In the authors' view, why would companies that develop animal organs for human transplantation be ethically justified in selling and profiting from their products?

Xenotransplantation involves the transplantation of organs, tissues, or cells from one species to another. Of major interest, of course, is transplantation from animals into humans, which has enormous potential to fulfill the demand for transplantable organs, tissues and cells to alleviate disease and save human lives. Initially, the ideal source animals were thought to be nonhuman primates, since these are close to humans phylogenetically and therefore represent the best immunological match. However, for a number of reasons, current opinion [as of 2005] now favours the use of the pig as the source animal. Biotechnology is developing rapidly, which it is hoped will enable us to overcome the many immune-related and other difficulties that xenotransplantation presents. The prospect that this form of surgical therapy will become a clinical reality is drawing closer. . . .

It should not be forgotten that xenotransplantation would render obsolete the numerous ethical questions relating to human allotransplantation (transfer of organs, tissues or cells between individuals of the same species). These include the illegal trade in the sale of organs from living donors, the use of condemned prisoners as donors in some countries, and the

Pig-to-Human Transplants Are on the Horizon

Thousands of patients die every year in the United States waiting for a suitable donor organ. So surgery professor David Sachs has been trying to figure out how to successfully put a pig organ into a primate. The Massachusetts General Hospital researcher and clinician thinks he has almost found the right protocol: a combination of organs from miniaturized, genetically engineered pigs and pig immune tissue that can prime the primate immune system to accept foreign parts.

The longest any animal has survived such a transplant is 83 days, still far short of the one-year survival time that Sachs, director of the Transplantation Biology Research Center at MGH, considers a benchmark to start human trials. But he thinks with a few minor tweaks, the procedure will be ready to try in patients, possibly in as little as five years.

Emily Singer, "Pig-to-Human Transplants on the Horizon,"
Technology Review, *October 10, 2006.*

controversial question of whether living donors or the families of deceased donors should receive financial rewards for their donation. . . .

Minimizing Risks of Animal-to-Human Virus Transfer

Apart from the inherent risks associated with the introduction of any new form of medical therapy, the one specific risk of xenotransplantation that has gained most attention is that of the transfer of a porcine infectious agent to the human organ recipient, and more importantly, from the recipient to his/her family, friends, and medical attendants.

There are, however, several advantages in this respect to be gained from xenotransplantation. First, the organ will be retrieved from a pig whose health status has been thoroughly monitored and is fully known, in marked contrast to the human organ donor. If an infectious agent is inadvertently present in the pig at the time of transplantation, it is possible that it is with a species-specific microorganism, which will not be of risk to the recipient. For example, strains of cytomegalovirus are species-specific (i.e., the strain only infects a specific species, e.g., pigs, and is unable to infect other species, e.g., humans). In experimental models, there has been no transfer of porcine cytomegalovirus from the transplanted pig organ to the nonhuman primate recipient.

Steps are being taken to breed herds of organ-source pigs that are free of all known infectious agents. From a risk assessment perspective, it would seem reasonable and acceptable to transplant organs from pigs in which the presence of all known [outside infectious] organisms of significance has been excluded. To delay a clinical trial because of the potential risk of unknown microorganisms would seem illogical, since there will always be an "unknown" to any scientific endeavour.

Nevertheless, the possibility of the transmission of a porcine endogenous retrovirus (PERV) may persist. Porcine endogenous retroviruses are viruses or virus particles that have existed in the nucleus of all pig cells for thousands, if not millions, of years. Although they appear to do the pig no harm, and their human counterparts do humans no harm, there is concern that infection of human cells by pig viruses may be pathogenic and lead to conditions such as immunodeficiency or malignancy. However, there is no current evidence that they will be pathogenic, and with modern biotechnology it is possible that pigs that are free of PERV may be produced within the next few years. . . .

The Issue of Animal Rights

[Another issue] is whether we can ethically justify the use of animals, and specifically pigs, for the purpose of xenotransplantation.

Human attitudes towards animals have changed greatly through the centuries, and still vary between cultures. Even within a given society, opinions extend from one extreme (that humans can treat animals as they wish) to the other (that animals have rights equal to those of humans). The middle-of-the road view held by the majority is that animals should be treated humanely and with respect, but are not entitled to all the same rights as humans. Most of us would also accept that the more distant the species is from us phylogenetically (or in evolutionary terms), the fewer rights it has. (A notable exception is provided by endangered species, whose rights may increase substantially). Animal "rights" are usually taken to mean that the animal is entitled to be treated as we would treat our fellow human.

The concept has been put forward that a member of one species of animal is not necessarily inferior to a member of another species. For example, a healthy chimpanzee, who is an important social member of a group (or extended family) of chimpanzees and who demonstrates a degree of intelligence and emotion with which we can identify, may be a more "worthy" member of the world's animal kingdom than a severely brain-damaged human subject, who has been in a vegetative state for many years, or an anencephalic infant, who will never be aware that he or she is loved and will never be able to return that love.

Our ethical qualms relating to the use of the pig for such purposes are very much reduced in view of the fact that the pig is already purpose-bred as a source of food for humans. It may be that the general public will see this as a more acceptable use of animals than simply as a food source, and readily see its benefit to mankind. Physicians have used heart valves from pigs, animal products, such as insulin, and animal tissue, such as skin grafts, for burnt patients, for many years. The use of animals for these forms of treatment has generally been accepted by the public. . . .

Today, there continue to be differences of opinion regarding animal rights and certain practices which some people tolerate are not considered acceptable by others. However, there is broad acceptance of the use of pigs to provide food, insulin and heart valves for humans, and in all these cases the pig has to be killed, so those who do not object to the killing of pigs for these purposes should surely have no objection to killing pigs to provide whole organs for transplantation. If we can employ pig heart valves in large numbers, it is surely nonsensical to object to the use of pig hearts. Only extreme vegetarians (who do not eat any form of animal tissue, do not wear leather shoes, etc.) can reasonably raise objections to the use of the pig in xenotransplantation.

Those who breed pigs for organ donation will be regulated by various government bodies to ensure that the animals receive proper care and housing. The high quality of the end product—the donor organs—will be essential if such breeders are to remain in business. Since the livelihood of the breeders will depend on their raising healthy pigs, the animals will be raised under ideal conditions that will certainly exceed those of all farm animals (and even some humans). Indeed, it is unlikely that any animals will ever have been maintained so carefully, with the possible exception of valuable racehorses. . . .

The Issue of Commercialization

The pigs used as a source of organs for xenotransplantation will undoubtedly be genetically engineered to render their organs resistant to the human immune response. Some believe that the genetic engineering of animals is little different from selective breeding. Indeed, genetic engineering allows us to achieve the desired goal much more rapidly, but it also allows us to breed genetically manipulated pigs that would be impossible to obtain by selective breeding. Pigs with human complement-regulatory proteins are one such example. . . .

If a transgenic pig is developed that plays a key role in the success of xenotransplantation, the question has been asked as to whether it is ethical for the company that breeds these pigs to make a profit from their sale. The view has been put forward that surely no profit should be derived from this humanitarian enterprise, just as blood and human organs should not be bought or sold for profit. Only the essential expenses involved in supplying the blood or organ should be passed on to the recipient or recipient organisation.

The key question is whether the pig organ should be grouped with human donor organs (which are, at least theoretically, provided to the recipients free of charge except for the expenses involved in their procurement), or with other lifesaving "devices" that have been developed by companies to be sold at a profit. The latter would include pig (and mechanical) heart valves, a multitude of drugs, as well as such equipment as dialysis machines and mechanical cardiac assist devices. All of these save lives, and it is not thought wrong to make a profit from their development and sale. The companies that develop transgenic pigs will expect to make a reasonable profit from their investment of time, money, and resources, and this should surely not be considered in any way unethical or unjustified.

| "There is no way to ensure that xeno might not kill many more people than it could save."

Animal-to-Human Organ Transplantation Is Unethical

Laura Purdy

Laura Purdy raises four ethical objections to xenotransplantation—animal-to-human organ transplants—in the following viewpoint. First, she argues, there is no public consensus on the morality of breeding and killing animals for their organs. Second, estimates of how many people would actually accept animal organs may be exaggerated. Third, consent to transplant surgery cannot truly be informed, because no one knows what harmful consequences to the patient might follow. Finally, she contends, the risk of cross-species disease transmission threatens the public at large, who have no say in the consent process. Purdy advocates alternative responses to the organ shortage, primarily increasing human donation and reducing the unhealthy lifestyle choices that lead to organ failure in the first place. Laura Purdy is professor of philosophy and Ruth and Albert Koch Professor of Humanities at Wells College in Aurora, New York, and the author of Bioethics, Justice, and Health Care.

Laura Purdy, "The Case Against Xenotransplantation," *Philosophy Now*, no. 55, May–June 2006, www.philosophynow.org. Copyright © Laura Purdy 2006. Reproduced by permission.

As you read, consider the following questions:

1. Why do people who accept killing animals for food object to killing them for xenotransplantation research, according to Purdy?

2. What burdensome restrictions would xeno patients be unlikely to comply with for the rest of their lives, in the author's opinion?

3. What causes of organ failure does Purdy suggest public-health campaigns should address as an ethical alternative to xenotransplantation?

Why not go full steam ahead with [xenotransplantation] research? Alas, free lunches are in short supply, and xeno is no exception. Several major moral issues need to be resolved before proceeding. What about animal rights and animal welfare? Would people accept animal organs? Could standards of informed consent be maintained? Last, does the use of animal organs pose unreasonable threats to third parties? If so, are there good grounds for them (us) to accept such risks?. . .

Animal Issues

Xeno would be impossible without using animal materials, by definition. Do we have a right to use them?

Xeno *research* may be more problematic than any subsequent use of animals for organs. In current research, animals are both donors and recipients. Donor issues are similar to those that would arise once xeno is well established. But animal test recipients may be subjected to procedures that cause serious suffering. Some such suffering may be caused by the social context of the research: for example, profit-oriented research groups may perceive the demands of humane treatment of animals as obstacles to winning the race, not moral necessities. Even in the best circumstances, some suffering may be unavoidable: surgery causes pain, and drugs can cause a variety of seriously unpleasant symptoms. Donor animals may also suffer because of the conditions necessary for producing safe organs. To maintain a sterile environment, infant animals will be delivered by cesarean and kept isolated, causing much emotional suffering in social animals like pigs. However, the primary moral question that arises for donor animals is whether they (morally) may be killed for their donations.

Many people, including some scientists, regard these as trivial concerns. Although most believe that avoidable animal suffering and death should be prevented, their overriding concern is human welfare. Others believe that it could be morally acceptable to painlessly kill animals for human welfare, but that our aims do not justify animal suffering. Still others believe that it is wrong to do to animals what one wouldn't do to humans. . . .

It is important to notice that no *moral* conclusions about animals are *scientific*. That is, they depend on judgments about values, not about which means are best for achieving a particular goal. Scientists may be in a position to help the public understand what is at issue, but [they] have no special expertise in deciding how best to reason about competing values. Because these judgments implicate fundamental and deeply held beliefs, there needs to be full, honest, public discussion about what is proposed. This has not yet occurred.

Acceptability and Informed Consent

Acceptability and informed consent are two sides of the same coin. The first question is whether candidates for xeno would assent to the procedure. Xeno researchers assume that desperate people would gladly take any relevant organ. But studies suggest that might not be true. Some resistance might come from religious beliefs concerning this type of close relationship with non-human creatures. Some resistance might also come from realism concerning the risks and benefits of xeno.

Xeno Research Practices Are Inhumane and Unethical

Between 1994 and 2000, [British research laboratory] Imutran's researchers transplanted pig hearts and kidneys into hundreds of monkeys and baboons. In a bizarre effort to bypass several million years of evolutionary difference between pigs and primates, Imutran scientists, with backing from their masters at Novartis Pharma, invented experimental cocktails of powerful immunosuppressants to try to stop the natural rejection of the fundamentally 'foreign' organs. The spleens were removed from many monkeys to further weaken their immune systems. The consequences were truly horrific.

Having survived captivity and a long, dangerous journey, a quarter of the primates died from 'technical failures'—jargon for lethal shortcomings in the experimental surgery . . .

If the monkeys and baboons survived surgery, they then faced an inevitable, traumatic death from one or a combination of these factors: organ rejection and failure, infections resulting from severely impaired immune systems, and/or drug toxicity. For example, kidney failure results in an accumulation of waste products such as urea in the blood. This in turn leads to nausea, vomiting, lethargy, listlessness, swelling, huddling in pain, drowsiness, anorexia and eventually death.

Dan Lyons, "Diaries of Despair,"
Uncaged Campaigns, *2003.*

The second issue is whether candidates for xeno could ever provide fully informed voluntary consent. Such consent is difficult enough to obtain from seriously ill patients for whom any invasive treatment is proposed. The special problems associated with xeno exacerbate these difficulties. . . .

Informed consent for xenotransplantation raises its own questions. On the one hand, it is hard to be very precise about what could go wrong and what patients would experience with such a new technology. On the other, patients and their intimates must be prepared to consent to intrusive and demanding conditions because of potential risks to third parties. Among the conditions that have been proposed are lifelong monitoring, using barrier methods or contraception, reporting sexual partners, educating close contacts about risk, refraining from childbearing, and accepting quarantine in case of infection. The 2003 SARS epidemic suggests that plenty of people will be ready to flout voluntary quarantine guidelines. Will democratic societies take stronger measures to protect the public in case xenotransplantation goes wrong?

Risk of Disease Transmission

The most distinctive xeno problem is in fact, this risk of disease transmission to third parties. This is a problem that changes a decision to pursue xeno research and treatment from a private matter to a public one about justice. . . .

Scientists are now attempting to determine whether pig pathogens might infect humans. However, the studies involve small samples and are short-term. Thus even negative results don't necessarily reflect the real danger. The underlying problem is that judgments about risk are inductive. But no matter how many 'safe' results accumulate, the very next case might reveal catastrophic infection. Although it may be tempting to dismiss this point as trivial, that would be a serious mistake. If technical obstacles to xeno such as organ rejection can be overcome, and the practice becomes widespread, no obvious disease might emerge for years. But even an extremely low risk could eventually produce something like AIDS, or worse. Consider, for instance, a cancer-causing herpes virus that spreads in the air.

Two additional risk factors should give us still more pause. One is that transplants—any transplant—now requires the recipient's immune system to be suppressed, otherwise an organ perceived as alien would be rejected. But this immuno-suppressed environment encourages bacteria and viruses to flourish, unchecked by the host's defense mechanisms. More-over, if animals intended as sources for xeno are engineered with human genes, their microbes will have a chance to become adapted to the human environment while still 'at home' in their animal hosts. That state of affairs would make it harder for our human immune systems to crush them. In short, as one writer has suggested, if you wanted to design an environment for creating new diseases, xeno would be ideal.

Instead, Seek Alternatives to Xeno

These facts suggest that there is no way to ensure that xeno might not kill many more people than it could save. So despite its promise, I believe that we should instead seek alternative ways to address the problem it is intended to fix. . . .

The central question is how to diminish the gap between the low supply of organs and the high demand for them. The obvious first step would be to universally apply the most successful strategies for increasing donation rates, and to develop new ones. Another step would be to apply other existing treatments and develop others. Existing treatments might rescue some who now face organ failure; for example some treatments, such as heart assist devices, currently considered as bridges to transplant, are showing promising signs of providing sufficient respite for damaged organs to repair themselves. New technologies such as tissue engineering also show promise. Astoundingly, researchers have already constructed a functioning dog bladder. And, the potential of stem cells is still unknown, but perhaps revolutionary.

Preventing disease in the first place would be best, naturally. Yet some cases of organ failure are caused by accidents

Periodical Bibliography

The following articles have been selected to supplement the diverse views presented in this chapter.

K. A. Bramstedt and Jun Xu	"Checklist: Passport, Plane Ticket, Organ Transplant," *American Journal of Transplantation*, July 2007.
Gerald D. Coleman	"Organ Donation: Charity or Commerce?" *America*, March 5, 2007.
Cosmopolitan	"I Chose to Share My Donated Liver," July 2007.
Peter Coy and Eric	"Organ Donor Economics," *Business Week*, February 5, 2007.
Tom Cunneff	"A Mother's Gift," *People Weekly*, December 5, 2005.
Kimberly Davis	"Organ Donations: The Power of Second Chances," *Ebony*, July 2005.
Essence	"The Gift of Life," January 2005.
Thomas Fields-Meyer	"Can a New Heart Change Your Life?" *People Weekly*, April 4, 2005.
Calixto Machado, et al.	"The Concept of Brain Death Did Not Evolve to Benefit Organ Transplants," *Ethics*, April 2007.
Damian McNamara	"Skin Cancer Risk Rises After Organ Transplant," *Family Practice News*, May 15, 2005.
Laura Meckler	"More Kidneys for Transplants May Go To Young," *Wall Street Journal*, March 10, 2007.
Richard C. Morais	"Desperate Arrangements," *Forbes Global*, January 29, 2007.

Is Human Genetic Testing Ethical?

Chapter Preface

One of the concerns held by those who object to human genetic testing is the fear that history may repeat itself. Representations of driven scientists who cooperate with questionable governments to develop a master race to dominate the world are not just fantastical yarns in science fiction books and Hollywood movies. There are many painful lessons in the history of various eugenics movements about the misuse of genetic information for ghastly purposes, including mistreating or murdering people because of beliefs about their genes.

The term eugenics was coined in 1883 by the British scientist Francis Galton who was a cousin of Charles Darwin. Galton believed that people born into the upper classes were endowed with superior inherited qualities that enabled them to achieve economic, social, and political success. Those born poor and in the working class were biologically inferior. Galton regarded the social or economic environment that people were born into as insignificant; a person's biology was their destiny. Scientists who agreed with Galton achieved considerable popular approval in many different countries by the early 20^0 century. In the United States, eugenic ideas led to immigration laws banning those thought to be inferior from entering the country. They also justified involuntary sterilization laws that prevented citizens thought to have defective genes from reproducing.

Perhaps the most notorious example of the misuse of genetic information occurred in Nazi Germany. Adolf Hitler's government exploited the long-festering tensions among majority and minority groups and encouraged eugenic ideas about the superiority of the "Aryan race." As Hitler rose to power, laws were passed permitting compulsory sterilization of people deemed unfit to propagate. Then policies took hold that demanded the euthanizing of children with serious physical or mental illness. Next, Hitler's "T-4" program systematically exterminated disabled and chronically ill adults. The final outcome of Hitler's eugenic plan for Jewish people is well known. Over six million Jews were killed in the Nazi concentration camps. Less well known is that around 100,000 mentally ill adults and children, between 90,000 and 220,000 gypsies, between 5,000 and 15,000 gay men, and over 85,000 Freemasons and Jehovah's Witnesses were also murdered. All of these groups were deemed genetically inferior and therefore a threat to the purity of the "Aryan race."

The cautionary history of Nazi Germany and other eugenics movements inspires those who are skeptical about genetic testing to call for close scrutiny of the goals and uses of genetic research. Many have concerns that without close supervision and independent oversight, dangerous applications of genetic testing can contaminate the beneficial possibilities of leading-edge science.

| *"Prenatal testing [gives] families the option of selecting against the genetic abnormalities of their choice and the freedom to construct their families as they choose."*

Fetal Genetic Testing Is Ethical

Robert J. Boyle and Julian Savulescu

Fetal genetic testing cannot be ethically prohibited in modern society, Robert J. Boyle and Julian Savulescu argue in the following viewpoint. According to Boyle and Savulescu, parents decide for many different personal reasons to end or continue pregnancies, and as long as they have that right, then prenatal diagnosis (PND) and preimplantation genetic diagnosis (PGD) are not unethical just because the results might turn out to be one of those reasons. The authors further claim that for society to dictate which genetic abnormalities may be selected against and which may not amounts to coercive eugenic practice. Robert J. Boyle is a geneticist at the Murdoch Children's Research Institute in Victoria, Australia. Julian Savulescu is Uehiro Professor of Practical Ethics at the University of Oxford.

Robert J. Boyle and Julian Savulescu, "Prenatal Diagnosis for 'Minor' Genetic Abnormalities Is Ethical," *American Journal of Bioethics*, vol. 3, no. 1, winter 2003, pp. 60–65. Reproduced by permission of Taylor & Francis Group, LLC, www.taylorandfrancis.com.

As you read, consider the following questions:

1. According to Boyle and Savulescu, how many conditions can be detected by genetic testing technologies?

2. How do the authors dispute the claim that selecting against a fetus with a genetic abnormality stigmatizes people living with the same genetic condition?

3. What two fetal testing procedures have been routinely performed for decades to get fetal health and genetic information, without ethical objections, according to the authors?

We argue that in a society where couples have considerable autonomy relating to decisions about the fetus at least until viability, the routine restriction of [prenatal diagnosis] PND for minor genetic abnormalities would be an unjust infringement of individual liberty.

Over 22,000 mutations have been identified in human genes and the number of recognized genetic disorders increases each year. Even the commonest genetic disorders are rare, but together they affect around 2% of births. Minor genetic variations with health implications are even more common—for example Factor V Leiden, which predisposes to venous thrombosis, is present in up to 12% of people in some countries—and every one of us carry mutations which have the potential to cause genetic disorders in our children.

Genetic testing is available for over 800 conditions and such testing may be used prenatally to detect severe or less severe disorders. . . .

An important question in PND is whether women should be allowed complete autonomy over which prenatal tests they request regarding the health of their fetus. . . .

Is Testing Discriminatory?

There is controversy over the degree to which PND is discriminatory—discriminatory against the unborn child with a genetic abnormality and against those alive with the same genetic condition. One of us has argued that allowing access to termination of pregnancy on the basis of perceived severity of fetal abnormality constitutes a form of discrimination and unacceptable eugenics. Since we all carry recessive mutations, the stigmatising effect of allowing selection against carrier state or minor genetic abnormalities is likely to be less than the stigmatising effect or the current choice to select against clinically apparent genetic disorders. . . .

There is a theoretical risk that by the widespread selection of fetuses based on their genetic make up we may risk affecting the genetic mix of our species and exposing the human race to unforeseen risks. However Haemophilia carriers [for example] are not known to have a survival advantage and indeed may occasionally suffer minor bleeding problems. The probability of Haemophilia mutations or other minor genetic abnormalities conferring a significant survival advantage is low in a world where technology and lifestyle modification play a major role in influencing lifespan and susceptibility to disease. The number of such requests is likely to be limited, and with this in mind reduced genetic diversity is not of great enough concern to warrant interference in this area of private decision-making.

In practice in much of Europe, Australia and the United States until 'viability' (usually 24 weeks gestation) any rights the fetus may be said to have are secondary to those of the pregnant woman. The fetus may however have some limited rights, as reflected by the restrictions regarding experimentation on human embryos. It is conceivable that where PND and termination is requested for genetic abnormalities of little significance to the fetus (albeit of concern to the pregnant woman) then these fetal rights may become relevant and pro-

> ## Eradicating Disease in Future Generations
>
> Today, using a scientific advance called preimplantation genetic diagnosis (PGD), couples can create embryos through standard fertility methods, then screen them for genetic disorders, selecting only those that are mutation-free for implantation. The practice is expensive (in the tens of thousands of dollars) and not widespread, but a 2006 survey of fertility clinics by the Genetics and Public Policy Center found that 28 percent [of the clinics] have used PGD to help couples avoid diseases that strike in adulthood, like breast cancer and Huntington's. Kari and Tim Baker knew they had to give it a try. Kari's grandfather died of Huntington's, and her mother was diagnosed in 1999. Kari, a board member of the Huntington's Disease Society of America, wanted to spare her kids. Twins Brooklyn and Levi are now vibrant 2½-year-olds who will never have to worry. "There's great joy and peace in knowing we did everything we could to not pass this on," says Tim.
>
> Claudia Kalb, "Peering into the Future: Genetic Testing," *Newsweek, December 11, 2006.*

vide a basis to refuse the woman's request. However terminations of pregnancy for social indications are not subject to the same rigor—in practice if a woman is sufficiently concerned by the prospect of continuing a pregnancy then her concern is accepted and the reasons underlying it not explored in detail. To restrict the detection of even minor genetic variations in fetuses by PND while allowing indiscriminate termination of other healthy fetuses for poorly specified reasons would be unjust, unless a distinction can be made between these two forms of pregnancy selection. . . .

Not Enough Grounds to Draw a Line Between a Wanted and Unwanted Pregnancy

The ethical status of social terminations, where the pregnancy is not wanted under any circumstances may be viewed differently from that of terminations subsequent to PND, where prior to PND the pregnancy is 'wanted'. But such a distinction is not clear—social terminations may in fact be for pregnancies that are initially *wanted*, but conditionally wanted and the conditions may change during the pregnancy. Or a woman having a termination for social reasons may wish to have a baby, but by a different man—her desire for a baby is conditional on who is the baby's father, that is on its genetic make up. Conversely pregnancies undergoing PND may be *unwanted* in the absence of PND—there is evidence that the availability of PND has increased pregnancy rates in families with Haemophilia A, and it is possible that refusal to provide genetic information about a pregnancy via PND may occasionally result in the termination of that pregnancy due to concerns about the possible genetic make up of the fetus. To draw a line between wanted and unwanted pregnancies is overly simplistic—many pregnancies are conditionally wanted, and that includes those terminated for personal reasons and those terminated following PND. It is difficult to draw a distinction between the ethics surrounding these two forms of pregnancy termination.

Harm to Society Has Not Been Demonstrated in Years of Use

If individual couples' requests for PND for minor abnormalities are to be restricted then such testing should first be shown to be harmful to society. Such testing may risk a conceptual shift in our attitude towards reproduction, children and the fetus. The practice of seeking 'designer babies' may be seen as eugenic practice at an individual family level, and as running the risk at a societal level of overemphasizing the genetic make up of our individuals. However information of minor consequence to a fetus' health is already routinely provided at antenatal ultrasound scanning (for example the sex of the fetus, or the presence of minor variations in physical parameters), and indeed selection of fetuses based upon their genetic makeup is commonplace. PND for the detection of chromosomal abnormalities (some of which may have only minor health implications) is chosen by many thousands of women each year. For society to dictate which genetic abnormalities are important enough to justify prenatal testing, to make some professional or societal value judgment that some genetic abnormalities are worth selecting against but others are not, has far more in common with the State run eugenic practices of the last century than giving families the option of selecting against the genetic abnormalities of their choice and the freedom to construct their families as they choose. The onus is upon those who oppose PND for minor genetic abnormalities to show that there is a clear harm to society caused by allowing these women access to such information about their fetus.

Preimplantation Genetic Diagnosis

PGD is a relatively new technique that involves the genetic analysis of artificially fertilised embryos (at around the 8 cell stage) so as to select a desired genotype prior to embryo implantation. The potential demand for minor genetic information at PGD may be greater than that for similar information by PND since in vitro fertilization (IVF) frequently produces excess embryos and selection among these embryos is necessary. Moreover, the costs of selection in the case of IVF are much less—the psychological burden of termination of established pregnancy is not present. This means that the implications of using PGD to prevent minor genetic abnormalities would be greater for society in terms of both resources and the effect on genetic diversity. However this technique is still likely to be used in only a small minority of pregnancies given its economic, physical and emotional implications for the couple. Any impact on genetic diversity is unlikely to be significant. To date little over 2,500 cycles of PGD have been completed worldwide, whereas over 18,000 amniocenteses are performed each year in the UK alone, mostly for PND or a chromosomal abnormality. The objections to testing for carrier status are also weaker in PGD, where there are already several embryos only some of which are to be implanted. Resource implications are likely to limit the use of PGD solely to detect minor genetic abnormalities, at least within a public health service. However if it is being employed anyway for the selection of an embryo without a specific genetic disease, there seems little reason not to select an embryo who isn't a carrier either if that is what the couple wishes.

Aside from considerations of the fair allocation of scarce resources, there is no good reason to routinely restrict either PND or PGD for the detection of minor genetic abnormalities in a society where the termination of healthy fetuses early in pregnancy is largely unrestricted. . . .

For the moment, we should be offering prenatal tests for minor genetic conditions or else fall into the trap of interfering in individual liberty for no good reason.

> *"With genetic screening, procreation be-*
> *gins to take on certain aspects of the*
> *idea—if not the practice—of manufac-*
> *ture, the making of a product to a*
> *specified standard."*

Fetal Genetic Testing Is Unethical

Samuel D. Hensley

In the following viewpoint, physician Samuel D. Hensley con-
demns fetal genetic testing on ethical and religious grounds. In
Hensley's opinion, prenatal testing to identify genetic defects
(and presumably end the pregnancy) and pre-implantation ge-
netic diagnosis (PGD) to identify desirable traits (designing ba-
bies for parental use or satisfaction) both completely disregard
the welfare and rights of the unborn child, and both amount to
playing God. Samuel D. Hensley is a surgical pathologist at Mis-
sissippi Baptist Medical Center in Jackson, Mississippi, and assis-
tant clinical professor at the University of Mississippi School of
Medicine. He is a fellow of the Center for Bioethics and Human
Dignity, which considers Christian perspectives in the scientific
and ethical debate over biomedical technologies.

As you read, consider the following questions:

1. What Christian argument does Hensley advance to support his view that PGD is unethical?

2. What non-Christian argument by philosopher Immanuel Kant does the author use to support his view that PGD is unethical?

3. According to Hensley, why is blastomere biopsy medically as well as ethically risky?

A [2004] *USA Today* article describes the difficulties of Joe Fletcher and his family in Northern Ireland. Joe's son, Joshua, has Diamond-Blackfan anemia, a condition that usually occurs as a spontaneous genetic mutation. If the affected individual reaches reproductive age, the trait is usually heritable as an autosomal [any chromosome other than a sex-determining chromosome] dominant disease. Joshua must receive repeated blood transfusions to counteract his inability to produce red blood cells, which carry oxygen to various parts of the body. The only cure for this condition is a stem cell transplant from a compatible donor. Joshua's older brother is not a compatible donor and the chance of any other future siblings being compatible is one in four. The Fletchers hope to improve those odds significantly by using a technique known as *pre-implantation genetic diagnosis* (PGD). The process requires in vitro fertilization. Eggs and sperm from the parents are mixed in a petri dish, and the resulting embryos undergo DNA analysis. Embryos compatible with Joshua could be inserted into the mother's womb to produce compatible siblings. Alternatively, if only a few embryos are compatible, they could be cloned to produce additional embryos in case the first attempt fails to result in implantation and fetal development.

Testing Turns Persons into Instruments

This procedure is illegal in Great Britain and is regarded as unethical. Why? Before exploring the British objection, let me add an additional concern from a Christian perspective that regards these embryos as early human life, made in the image of God, possessing unique genes and the capability of continued human development. An important question for Christians is what will happen to the healthy embryos that are incompatible with Joshua. Will they be implanted later and given an equal chance at continued life or will they be discarded? Embryos not selected may be destroyed directly or by destructive embryo research, which is contrary to an understanding of human life being sacred. The *USA Today* article does not mention what plans the parents have for these other offspring.

The British concern expressed previously by the Human Fertilization and Embryology Authority (HFEA) is that human life would be created for the purpose of benefiting others, in this case a brother and the parents. This is a serious ethical concern. Should a child be created specifically to save another person's life, or should a child be welcomed and loved unconditionally regardless of his or her instrumental value in helping someone else? This is important not just from a Christian perspective. Immanuel Kant, the prominent philosopher of rationalism, felt that human beings should always be treated as ends in themselves and not as the means for another person to attain his or her ends. In the Fletcher case, it does not seem that the embryos would be screened to test for known genetic defects. If Diamond-Blackfan anemia is a spontaneous mutation, and no known genetic anomalies are detectable in the parents (such as a mutation for RPS 19 on chromosome 19), then genetic screening is not a helpful option. The decision on life or death then would be made solely on whether a particular embryo, at a later stage of life, might be useful in helping Joshua. This pushes the issue of creating life to serve our needs and wants to a new level, and raises the issue of designer babies.

Are We Willing to Prevent a Future Bill Gates or Thomas Jefferson from Being Born?

What if I told you it's possible that [Bill] Gates has a medical condition that accounts, in part, for both his tremendous achievements and for his "nerdiness?" Gates is widely reported to display many personality traits characteristic of a condition known as Asperger's syndrome. Asperger's is a mild version of autism, a more serious condition that renders many children unable to talk, be touched, communicate or socialize. While I certainly do not know if Gates has Asperger's, his difficulties in social settings are nearly as legendary as his genius, so it's possible. . . .

There is a good chance we will soon have a genetic test for detecting the risk of autism in an embryo or fetus. The development of such a screening tool raises the possibility that parents might one day have the option of preventing the birth of a child with even a mild case of the disorder. . . .

There are many in the autism and Asperger's community, like the newly formed Aspies for Freedom, who worry that the minute a genetic test appears, it will spell the end for a lot of future geniuses, like Gates. Maybe there will be fewer Thomas Jeffersons or Lewis Carrolls—remarkable thinkers who also fit the profile for Asperger's.

Arthur Caplan, "Would You Have Allowed Bill Gates to Be Born?"
MSNBC.com, *May 31, 2005.*

Prenatal genetic testing allows scientists to test established pregnancies for genetic defects that then could be avoided by aborting the pregnancy. Pre-implantation genetic diagnosis allows multiple embryos to be tested and inserted into the mother only if certain *desirable* traits are present. This possibility was discussed by Dr. Francis Collins, director of the National Human Genome Research Institute, when he noted that the time may soon arrive when pre-implantation screening will be used to pick desirable traits even in the absence of particular genetic disorders. In the coming years, human genome research will delineate gene clusters associated with increased intelligence, athletic ability, and musicality to name a few. The temptation to redefine parenthood to include choosing particular characteristics in their children, as opposed to unconditionally accepting offspring as a gift of God, seems fraught with perils beyond the scope of this article. For the sake of reflection, let us briefly consider a few issues.

Blastomere biopsy, the process by which a single cell is taken from the embryo for genetic testing, seems safe, but no long-term studies are available to exclude later problems from the procedure itself. In medical research, when new therapies are tested on human subjects, the welfare of the patient is a paramount concern. However, with in vitro fertilization, blastomere biopsy, and genetic screening, the embryos are not considered human subjects even though they are the earliest forms of childhood development and the beginning of lives whose health and well-being will later be a concern to all. Safety for the embryo must be a vital concern.

Testing Turns Procreation into Manufacture

Our culture has generally considered parents to be the best judges of the welfare of their offspring, but even this has limits. Children are weak and vulnerable; they require protection from abuse and negligence. The ability for parents to choose which offspring die and which live and what traits they will manifest is an awesome responsibility. The President's Council of Bioethics recently noted that

> With genetic screening, procreation begins to take on certain aspects of the *idea*—if not the practice—of manufacture, the making of a product to a specified standard. The parent—in partnership with the IVF doctor or genetic coun-

selor—becomes in some measure the master of the child's fate, in ways that are without precedent ... Today, parents using PGD take responsibility for selecting for birth children who will not be chronically sick or severely disabled; in the future, they might also bear responsibility for picking and choosing which "advantages" their children shall enjoy. Such an enlarged degree of parental control over the genetic endowments of their children cannot fail to alter the parent-child relationship. Selecting against disease merely relieves the parents of the fear of specific ailments afflicting their child; selecting for desired traits inevitably plants specific hopes and expectations as to how their child might excel. More than any child does now, the "better" child may bear the burden of living up to the standards he was "designed" to meet. The oppressive weight of his parents' expectations—resting in this case on what they believe to be undeniable biological facts—may impinge upon the child's freedom to make his own way in the world.

These concerns for tomorrow begin with Joshua's parents today. The proposal is to select purposefully a child solely for his ability to provide a donor source for another child. Creating life primarily to serve someone else, especially when the other life may be rejected and destroyed for the simple reason that it did not meet the parents' needs, is an action that should always be condemned.

> *"Is it ever ethically* mandatory *for employers to offer genetic testing? We believe that it is."*

Genetic Testing in the Workplace Can Be Ethical

Chris MacDonald and Bryn Williams-Jones

Although forced genetic testing in the workplace may not be ethically permissible, Chris MacDonald and Bryn Williams-Jones argue in the following viewpoint that employers ethically can (and in some cases must) offer genetic testing to would-be and current employees. Testing would detect susceptibility to workplace toxins and reduce costs associated with occupational disease: MacDonald and Williams-Jones contend this is ethical if the test is specific, reliable, free, and confidential; if it doesn't target any particular population group; and if it doesn't unfairly threaten employees' jobs. Chris MacDonald is a bioethicist with an interest in business and professional ethics at Dalhousie University in Nova Scotia. Bryn Williams-Jones, an assistant professor in the Bioethics Program of the University of Montreal, researches the ethics of commercial genetic testing.

Chris MacDonald and Bryn Williams-Jones, "Ethics and Genetics: Susceptibility Testing in the Workplace," *Journal of Business Ethics*, vol. 35, 2002, pp. 235–41. Copyright © 2002 Kluwer Academic Publishers. Reproduced by permission.

As you read, consider the following questions:

1. What two genes, for example, are known to make people more susceptible to disease if exposed to certain workplace hazards, according to Mac-Donald and Williams-Jones?

2. If genetic testing meets the ethical conditions set by the authors, how would it benefit employees as well as employers?

3. When is it mandatory for employers to offer genetic testing, in the authors' opinion?

Genetic screening can be used to detect which individuals have a genetic makeup associated with particular hereditary diseases, such as sickle cell anaemia, cystic fibrosis, and Huntington disease. Screening can also detect genes that confer increased susceptibility to workplace toxins or environmental factors, e.g., N-acetyltransferase phenotype (increased risk of bladder cancer in those exposed to carcinogenic arylamines) or Glu-69 (heightened susceptibility to beryllium, which can cause pulmonary disease).

Employers might benefit from genetic screening through reduction in costs associated with occupational disease, e.g., lost productivity, excess absenteeism, worker's compensation payments, health insurance premiums, and legal liability. While some tests are still relatively expensive, they will become more affordable as technologies develop and through cost savings from maintaining a healthy workforce. A further argument in favour of genetic screening is that in order to maintain a healthy and productive workforce and safeguard corporate interests, companies have to be selective about who they hire or retain as employees. It can be argued that companies are not unfairly discriminatory in selecting against employees at risk for hereditary disease or genetic susceptibility. Workplace discrimination is generally not thought to be unfair if the issue is a "bona fide" requirement of the job. And it may simply not

Genetic Testing Benefits the Employee as Well as the Employer

One argument [against genetic testing in the workplace] is that people will shy away from finding out their genetic position if they are subject to the test. Don't believe all this. By assumption, there is good reason to believe that the information that is acquired from genetic sources is of value not only to the employer but also to the employee. Suppose that a women has the gene that renders her susceptible to breast cancer, which if identified would allow for certain prophylactic choices. Does it really make sense to think that she would choose not to get that information if she had to disclose it to a prospective employer? Hard to believe that workers would take that kind of risk with their own lives. The point is doubly true because nothing says that the worker has to disclose a genetic condition and just stop. She is always allowed to add further information which indicates the steps that have been taken to counteract that risk, so as to allay the fears of an employer. The last thing that we need for these key decisions is less information than more.

Richard A. Epstein, "Two Cheers for Genetic Testing,"
University of Chicago Law School Faculty Blog, *October 18, 2005.*

be economically feasible for the employer to eliminate all substances that put a few hypersensitive employees at risk. It may be more sensible, from an economic point of view, not to hire susceptible workers or to transfer susceptible workers to different positions. Finally, if challenged that using genetic screening in the workplace is unfairly discriminatory, employers can reply that prospective (and current) employees do not have a right to work at a specific company, and that those who object to screening can seek employment elsewhere....

Those in favour of [workplace] genetic screening are probably justified in citing employee benefit, corporate responsibility, and economics as reasons for using genetic testing to select against certain employees while protecting those already employed who may be susceptible. Opponents to screening also provide persuasive arguments for the need for concern about justice and discrimination, scientific validity, and privacy. . . .

Given that workplace genetic testing is a technology both full of promise and fraught with ethical peril, we suggest a pragmatic approach that allows for the possibility of workplace genetic testing, but that attempts to minimize its negative effects. Each of the positive and negative factors alluded to above warrants serious ethical investigation. . . . We propose a set of criteria, the satisfaction of which would make it *prima facie* permissible for employers to offer genetic testing to workers. *Requiring* workers to submit to genetic testing is significantly more problematic morally. Forced testing would constitute an invasion of privacy and expose the worker—on a nonvoluntary basis—to a range of poorly understood risks. Thus, it may not be possible to identify circumstances in which such a requirement would be ethically permissible. We do not attempt that task here. As a result, we restrict our discussion to the search for conditions under which it would be permissible for employers to offer employees the *opportunity* to be tested. We contend that it is *ethically permissible* to offer genetic testing to employees if the following six conditions are met:

1. A genetic test (for a specific condition) must be available which is highly specific and sensitive and offers an acceptably low incidence of both false positives and false negatives; such a test must test for a gene that is sufficiently penetrant for the test result to have some important health implication.

2. Testing should be carried out by an independent lab, and results of genetic tests should be given to

workers directly, either by a geneticist or a genetic counsellor; test results should be held confidential, and revealed to the employer only at the employee's request;

3. Pre- and post-test genetic counselling must be available from a qualified health professional, and paid for by the employer, regardless of the outcome of the test;

4. The gene being tested for must not be prominently associated with an identifiable and historically disadvantaged group;

5. Where relevant, the employer must guarantee continued access to group insurance;

6. The employer must ensure that if the employee chooses to reveal that she has tested positive, suitable policies are in place to ensure a reasonable degree of job security.

We feel that if the above criteria were met, it would be ethically permissible to offer (but not to *require*) workplace genetic testing. Meeting these criteria would allow employers to offer genetic testing, and further to have reasonable answers in the face of most of the objections noted above. The only concern *not* directly addressed by meeting these six criteria is the worry that, in focusing on tailoring the workforce to the workplace environment (by using genetic testing to weed out those workers who are particularly susceptible to workplace hazards) employers may neglect improvements to the workplace that would benefit *all* employees. It would of course be possible to further stipulate that, in order for it to be permissible to offer genetic testing, employers must also ensure that other appropriate measures are taken to clean up the workplace so that the interests of "normal" workers as well as "at risk" workers are served. We feel, however, that the obligation to provide a safe workplace for all employees is a general issue that can be separated from the issue of genetic testing.

If the six criteria above are met, then any genetic test that is offered holds the promise of being good for all involved. The employer reduces costs associated with employee illness; at-risk employees gain the information needed to remove themselves from work environments that pose special risks for them; and employees found *not* to be at increased risk gain the comfort of that knowledge. These advantages (in the absence of the disadvantages avoided through meeting our six criteria) justify offering testing. They do not justify failure to maintain a reasonably safe environment for all employees: employees found not to be at risk gain only psychological comfort from testing, and untested employees gain nothing at all from testing. The availability of testing does little if anything to change employers' health-and-safety related obligations to these employees.

Next, let us ask, is it ever ethically *mandatory* for employers to offer genetic testing? We believe that it is, and suggest that it be considered mandatory for an employer to offer genetic testing to employees if conditions 1 through 6 above are satisfied, and if, in addition, the following conditions are met:

1. Knowing their status with regard to the genetic characteristic in question can reasonably be expected to influence at least some employees' decision to remain in their current position;

2. The cost of the test is "reasonable" (e.g., is similar to the costs of other insured medical services, or other normal workplace benefits).

We think that the possibility of an obligation to offer testing to employees—and the financial burden that would imply—goes hand in hand with the possibility of *offering* genetic testing to employees, and the risks such testing would imply for them. In considering whether they favour a world in which

> "Excluding people from employment on the basis of their genetic make-up would constitute a violation of the fundamental human rights."

Genetic Testing in the Workplace Is Unethical

Rory O'Neill

Under no circumstances is genetic testing of prospective or current employees justifiable, according to Rory O'Neill in the following viewpoint. O'Neill argues that employers will use genetic testing unethically, to pick and choose employees to suit hazardous workplaces or to cut pension costs. Besides, he claims, genetic screening cannot accurately predict which workers will become sick or disabled, and discrimination is likely at every step of the testing process—already courts have struck down its use. Rory O'Neill is the editor of Hazards, *a British independent, pro-union quarterly that reports on workers' rights and workplace conditions.*

As you read, consider the following questions:

1. What preventive action should employers take instead of genetic testing to improve employees' health, according to O'Neill?

Rory O'Neill, "Gene Machine: Keep Your Hands Off Our Genes," *Hazards*, October–December 2003, http://hazards.org. Reproduced by permission.

2. Why is voluntary consent to genetic testing not truly voluntary in the workplace, in the author's opinion?

3. How did genetic testing of employees by Burlington Northern Santa Fe Railroad violate federal law, as described by O'Neill?

In recent years [as of 2003], genetic testing has become an affordable option, unregulated and used routinely by the police and increasingly common in our hospitals.

At work—where being at risk of an occupational disease isn't a crime or a personal trait, but the result of an exposure to an occupational risk—many, maybe most, UK employers are interested in using genetic screening as a scientific shortcut that could weed out the weak and cut compensation and sick leave.

An Institute of Directors report in 2000 found that 50 per cent of employers responding to a questionnaire thought it would be appropriate to conduct genetic testing "to see if employees are at risk of developing an occupation-related disease due to exposure in the workplace" and 34 per cent thought it would be appropriate "to see if they will develop heart disease which might affect sickness or early retirement."

One problem. They are wrong—where genetic testing has been used at work, it has been a disaster. In the US, where employers and insurers have been most enthusiastic for the tests, a 1997 survey found up to 10 per cent of firms might already be using gene screening. Equality chiefs have ruled it out of order and the government is on the verge of outlawing the practice entirely. . . .

Employers Should Make Workplaces Safe, Not Choose Workers Who Tolerate Hazards

A GeneWatch report, *Genetic Testing in the Workplace*, published on 25 September 2003, the day the Human Genetics Commission (HGC) met to consider the UK government's response to its recommendations on genetic discrimination, reveals that genetic tests cannot accurately predict which workers will suffer future disability or illness.

Despite this, many employers wish to use genetic test results and many research projects are seeking to identify people who are "genetically susceptible" to workplace hazards. It adds that workplace hazards affect everyone—not just people with "bad genes"—so the remaining workers would still be at risk.

"Some employers might see selecting workers on the basis of genetic tests simply as a more economic and efficient means of employee selection," says the report.

"Picking and choosing workers to suit hazardous environments or cut pensions costs is totally unacceptable," said Dr Helen Wallace, deputy director of GeneWatch UK. "The government should act now to close the loophole in the law. Worker exclusion must not replace employers' obligations to clean up workplaces for all.". . .

Gene Tests Don't Work

In 2001, *Hazards* warned of serious dangers in the use of genetic screening at work.

IT NEVER WORKED: Attempts in the 1960s to introduce workplace genetic screening were soundly rejected because occupational and environmental factors were a far more productive focus of preventive action;

IT STILL DOESN'T WORK: Efforts over 30 years to push gene screens for sensitivity to the potent workplace asthma cause TDI [toluene diisocyanate] and other substances have failed;

IT MISSES THE POINT: Genetic screening tended to give some—often dubious—protection from one risk. Many targeted substances including benzene, beryllium, lead and cadmium had many more and more serious risks for the entire workforce that would have been a better focus for "preventive" efforts; and

---

The Genetic Information Nondiscrimination Act of 2007 (GINA) Protects Employees Against Genetic Testing Abuses

SEC. 202. EMPLOYER PRACTICES.

(a) Discrimination Based on Genetic Information: It shall be an unlawful employment practice for an employer—

1. to fail or refuse to hire, or to discharge, any employee, or otherwise to discriminate against any employee with respect to the compensation, terms, conditions, or privileges of employment of the employee, because of genetic information with respect to the employee; or

2. to limit, segregate, or classify the employees of the employer in any way that would deprive or tend to deprive any employee of employment opportunities or otherwise adversely affect the status of the employee as an employee, because of genetic information with respect to the employee.

H.R. 493, passed by the House of Representatives, 110th Cong., 1st sess., April 25, 2007.

IT IS DISCRIMINATORY: The markers chosen were often linked to race—Sickle cell, Tay Sachs, Glucose-6-phosphate dehydrogenase (G-6-PD) deficiency—or gender, which could have led to something uncomfortably close to workplace eugenics.

Everybody Loses

The GeneWatch report warns that efforts to winnow out the weak or the susceptible are "fundamentally flawed."

The report says: "Genetic tests could result in many—perhaps hundreds—of workers being excluded to prevent one case of a workplace-related disease. The majority of those excluded would suffer the ill-effects of unemployment on their health and finances, even though they might not actually belong to a higher risk group." The report argues [the following points]:

There are more effective ways of improving employees' health—for example, meeting legal duties and ensuring risks are "eliminated, reduced or, at the every least, effectively controlled."

The imbalance of power between employer and employee makes it difficult to ensure that employees are giving their voluntary consent to a genetic test. Job applicants could face discrimination and existing workers might not be able to walk away from a high risk job, but could have the test used against them if they didn't leave the job and went on to develop an occupational disease.

A genetic test could have wider implications—for blood relatives who might have a similar genetic trait, or when applying for other jobs or for insurance.

The use of genetic tests is unethical—excluding people from employment on the basis of their genetic make-up would constitute a violation of their fundamental human rights.

The potential for discrimination—tests are complex and open to misinterpretation, can lead to "false positive" results, and [can] lead to a generally unemployable "genetic underclass."

For those with something to gain—the plethora of firms flogging testing kits for example, of the employers looking for a cut-price alternative to safe work—the your-money-or-your-life argument might have its attractions.

It seems unethical at best that 21st-century workplaces, where there is the capability to cheaply obtain a person's genetic fingerprint, can argue they can't make their workplaces safe.

Testers Face Legal Pitfalls

Where tests have been used, employers have sometimes found themselves on the wrong side of the law. In the US, legal, equal opportunity and governmental bodies have acted to curtail the practice.

In 2002, the US Equal Employment Opportunity Commission has told Burlington Northern Santa Fe Railroad that its use of secret genetic testing of some employees violated federal law.

An EEOC official said Burlington Northern broke the Americans with Disabilities Act by treating employees with carpal tunnel syndrome as disabled and then discriminating against them, and should pay compensation.

In December 2000, a US federal court approved a $2.2 billion settlement to thousands of employees of Lawrence Berkeley Laboratories who had been secretly tested for decades for syphilis, pregnancy and the genetic trait for sickle cell disease. . . .

Legislation Should Ban Workplace Testing

GeneWatch argues that your genetic fingerprint is personal, and not personnel, information. This argument appears to be winning in the US too where, despite the support of a powerful business and biotech lobby, genetic screening's days could be numbered.

In October 2003 the US Senate voted by overwhelming majority to approve legislation that would prohibit companies from using genetic test results to make employment decisions, deny health coverage or raise insurance premiums.

The measure, which will move forward for consideration by the House of Representatives, would bar insurers from requiring genetic tests, from obtaining test results, and from using the results of tests to increase insurance premiums or deny coverage. Employers would be barred from seeking most genetic information, and from using any such information to influence hiring or promotion decisions.

Employers could, however, require testing to monitor potential ill effects from workplace exposure to hazardous substances. And disability and workers' advocates warn that the proposed US law has employer-friendly loopholes—it would not, for example, rule out gene tests in occupational disease compensation cases, so the gene testers could still have a route into the workplace.

VIEWPOINT 5

> *"Even if life or health insurers were to . . . base underwriting decisions on genetic test results, the practice is unlikely to produce one class of genetically blessed and another class of genetically cursed individuals."*

Insurers Should Have Access to Genetic Testing Results

Neil A. Manson and Gregory Conko

Neil A. Manson and Gregory Conko have pointed out that once the link between cigarette smoking and lung cancer was discovered, life insurance companies legitimately started gathering information about their customers' tobacco use, splitting their customer pool into smokers and nonsmokers, and charging high-risk smokers higher premiums. In the following viewpoint, Manson and Conko argue that genetic testing is another legitimate way of gathering better information about their customers' health risks, so life insurers can offer low-risk people lower premiums and so people predisposed to some disease can change their behavior or environment to lower their risk (and improve their health—a win-win situation). Neil A. Manson is an assistant

Neil A. Manson and Gregory Conko, "Why the Fear of 'Genetic Discrimination' Does Not Justify Regulation," *Issue Analysis*, April 5, 2007. Copyright © 2007 Competitive Enterprise Institute. Reproduced by permission of Competitive Enterprise Institute (CEI).

professor of philosophy at the University of Mississippi. Gregory Conko is a senior fellow at the Competitive Enterprise Institute, a Washington, D.C., public policy group committed to free enterprise and limited government.

As you read, consider the following questions:

1. Why is new legislation regulating insurers' premium calculations and the use of genetic testing results unnecessary, in the authors' view?

2. What is wrong with studies that purportedly document genetic discrimination by insurance companies, according to Manson and Conko?

3. Why are genetic testing results of little value to health insurers, according to the authors?

It is common knowledge that many diseases have a genetic basis and that the presence of more and more disease-related genetic mutations can be detected with simple tests. Unfortunately, much of the American public believes that certain diseases are completely determined by one's genes and that a positive genetic test means doom. In turn, they fear that insurers will use information of such seemingly great predictive value to deny coverage to, or make insurance much more expensive for, those with positive genetic tests. Some also believe that employers may use genetic test information to discriminate against employees who are at greater risk of becoming ill. This has led to calls for government to regulate access to such information in order to prevent insurance companies and employers from engaging in what some have called "genetic discrimination."

Legislation Is Not Necessary

Fortunately, it is not true that carrying a genetic mutation for a given disease is a guarantee that the disease will eventually arise. Most genetic mutations only increase the probability of

Genetic Privacy Laws Allow High-Risk Insurees to Lie About Their Health

Preventing insurance companies from gaining access to the information provided by genetic tests leads to the problem of adverse selection. Adverse selection occurs when there is an asymmetry of information. In this case, people whose genetic tests indicate that they are at high risk of becoming ill or dying prematurely are likely to load up on gold-plated insurance coverage. Because insurers won't know the results of the tests, the premiums they charge will not cover the cost of taking care of high-risk customers.

In essence, genetic privacy laws allow high-risk insurees to lie about their health in order to get more money. This means that healthier customers will have to be charged more to pay for their high-risk counterparts. This situation can set off an adverse selection spiral in which low-risk clients flee the higher premiums and high-risk clients flock to buy the insurance.

Ronald Bailey, "Information Discrimination,"
Reason, *May 16, 2001.*

developing the disease, and most such diseases can be prevented or treated once the carrier knows about the mutation. Furthermore, it is already illegal for most health insurers to discriminate against potential customers on the basis of genetic test information. Nevertheless, members of Congress have introduced legislation to expand current laws that forbid health insurance providers from basing coverage or premium decisions on a customer's genetic status, and to forbid group health insurers from charging all members of a group plan higher rates based on the genetics of one or more members. The legislation would also prohibit employers from discriminating against individuals on the basis of genetic information.

Despite public perceptions, however, there is no strong evidence that genetic discrimination is currently a widespread problem, or that it is likely to become so in the future. Numerous investigations into actual underwriting practices show that neither health nor life insurers currently engage in such practices. The few studies that purportedly document genetic discrimination have not been sound methodologically. They rely solely on patient self-reports with no follow-up to confirm that genetic discrimination actually occurred. And most such studies give a misleading impression by defining use of family medical history in underwriting decisions as a form of "genetic discrimination." Ultimately, Dawn Allain, president of the National Society of Genetic Counselors, told the *Wall Street Journal* in 2004: "We haven't seen any real cases of genetic discrimination."

Of course, even though it is not occurring today, one might fear that genetic discrimination could become a genuine problem in the future, as scientists learn more about the genetic basis of many diseases. The economics of health insurance make it unlikely that those insurers will rely on genetic test information—at least for the foreseeable future. Most health insurance is provided by employers, and premiums for those plans are based on the experience of the insured group, not on the characteristics of any one member. In addition, health insurers tend to see a rapid turnover in enrollment, so trying to predict health problems that may or may not actually occur years into the future makes little sense.

More Information Could Result in Better Coverage

Life insurers, on the other hand, could, one day, have an incentive to use genetic test information, because their customers typically buy their policies individually and tend to keep the same insurer their whole lives. When practical, insurers can reduce the uncertainty in expected payouts by gathering better information about their customers' health risks. That helps policy holders because reducing such uncertainty lets the insurer reduce the financial cushion it needs to account for unknown high-cost customers within the insured group, leading to lower premiums.

Furthermore, even if life or health insurers were to find it practical to base underwriting decisions on genetic test results, the practice is unlikely to produce one class of genetically blessed and another class of genetically cursed individuals. Nearly all diseases with a genetic component can be prevented or treated with early detection, so widespread genetic testing is far more likely to result in improved health outcomes for most genetic diseases.

It is not even correct to assume that those genetically predisposed to some disease will have worse health outcomes when compared to the general population. In many cases, those armed with the knowledge that they are genetically predisposed to a given disease might well change their behaviors and control their environments sufficiently to gain a statistical edge over those not so genetically predisposed but who do not similarly alter their behavior. That could result in lower health or life insurance premiums. On the other hand, forbidding insurers from using genetic test results or other types of relevant information could restrict efficient underwriting and force all consumers to pay higher costs. Ultimately, arguments for increased government regulation of health and life insurers do not make economic or practical sense.

> *"Any proposed legislation must prohibit insurers from requiring, requesting, collecting, or buying genetic information about individuals who are covered or seeking coverage."*

Insurers Should Not Have Access to Genetic Testing Results

National Council on Disability

The National Council on Disability (NCD) is an independent federal agency that advises the president and Congress on issues affecting Americans with physical and mental disabilities and promotes integration of disabled Americans into all aspects of society. In the following viewpoint, the NCD reports evidence that health and life insurers, health care providers, blood banks, adoption agencies, the military, schools, and employers have all discriminated against asymptomatic people on the basis of genetic testing. Existing laws offer inadequate protections against this misuse, the NCD claims, and new legislation is needed that cuts off insurers' access to genetic information.

National Council on Disability, "Position Paper on Genetic Discrimination Legislation," March 4, 2002, www.ncd.gov.

233

As you read, consider the following questions:

1. What percentage of respondents to the *Science* magazine survey cited by the NCD reported that they or a family member were refused health insurance because of a genetic condition in the family?

2. Why are state laws insufficient against genetic testing discrimination, according to the NCD?

3. What is the only purpose for which the NCD says insurers may justifiably request information about an individual's genetic tests?

Discrimination based on genetic information is not a new phenomenon. During the early 1970s, employers used genetic screening to identify and exclude African Americans carrying a gene mutation for sickle cell anemia. These individuals were denied jobs despite the fact that many of them were healthy and never developed the disease. During the same time period, individuals who were carriers of sickle cell anemia were also discriminated against by several insurance companies despite the fact that they were asymptomatic.

Genetic Discrimination Is Systemic

Genetic discrimination by employers and insurers has continued to be a systemic problem. According to a 1989 survey conducted by Northwestern National Life Insurance Company, 15 percent of the companies surveyed indicated that by the year 2000, they planned to check the genetic status of prospective employees and their dependents before making employment offers.

A 1996 survey of individuals at risk of developing a genetic condition and parents of children with specific genetic conditions indicated more than 200 instances of genetic discrimination reported by the 917 respondents. The discrimination was practiced by employers, insurers, and other organizations. Another survey of genetic counselors, primary care physicians, and patients identified 550 individuals who were denied employment or insurance based on genetic information. A study on genetic discrimination, published in 1996, found that health and life insurance companies, health care providers, blood banks, adoption agencies, the military, and schools engaged in genetic discrimination against asymptomatic individuals.

Science magazine reported that in a study of 332 individuals with one or more family members with a genetic disorder who are affiliated with genetic support groups, 40 percent of the respondents recalled being specifically asked about genetic diseases or disabilities on their applications for health insurance. Twenty-two percent of the respondents said they or a family member were refused health insurance as a result of the genetic condition in the family. Fifteen percent of the respondents reported that they or affected family members had been asked questions about genetic diseases or disabilities on employment applications. Thirteen percent reported that they or a family member had been denied a job or fired from a job because of a genetic condition in the family, and 21 percent reported being denied a job or fired due to their own genetic disorder.

In addition to these and other studies, numerous anecdotal examples of genetic discrimination by employers and insurers have been detailed in testimony before Congress in hearings about genetic discrimination.

The misuse of genetic information not only excludes qualified individuals from employment and denies insurance coverage to individuals without justification, but also undercuts the fundamental purposes of genetic research. Such research has been undertaken with the goals of early identification, prevention and effective treatment of disease. These goals will be undermined if fear of discrimination deters people from genetic diagnosis and prognosis, makes them fearful of confiding in physicians and genetic counselors, and makes them more concerned with loss of a job or insurance than with care and treatment. . . .

Existing Laws Are Insufficient to Protect Individuals from Genetic Discrimination

There are existing laws that may prohibit genetic discrimination in some contexts. However, these laws do not reach much of the discrimination that occurs and, in some cases, may be interpreted not to apply to genetic discrimination at all.

The Americans with Disabilities Act (ADA), an anti-discrimination law, protects individuals who have an impairment that substantially limits them in a major life activity, who have a record of such an impairment, or who are regarded as having such an impairment. Congress intended ADA to cover individuals with a broad range of diseases, and some members of Congress explained at the time of ADA's passage that it would protect people who experience discrimination on the basis of predictive genetic information where those individuals were regarded as having a disability. . . .

Nonetheless, ADA is a highly problematic vehicle for fully addressing genetic discrimination. At 2002 Senate hearings, EEOC [Equal Employment Opportunity Commission] Commissioner Paul Steven Miller testified that while ADA could be interpreted to prohibit employment discrimination based on genetic information, it "does not explicitly address the issue and its protections are limited and uncertain.". . .

The Health Insurance Portability and Accountability Act (HIPAA) prohibits genetic discrimination by insurers in very limited circumstances. It prohibits group health plans from using any health status-related factor, including genetic information, as a basis for denying or limiting coverage or for charging an individual more for coverage. However, a plan may still establish limitations on the amount, level, extent or nature of benefits or coverage provided to similarly situated individuals. . . .

Insurers *Do* Discriminate on the Basis of Genetic Testing Results

Heidi Williams's two children were twice denied health insurance by the company Humana, because they were carriers of the genetic disorder alpha-1 antitrypsin deficiency, or AAT. Because the children had one normal and one abnormal copy of the gene, they would not have had any symptoms of the liver or lung disease that AAT causes. It was only when the media became involved in the issue that Humana reversed its decision. "Humana, Inc. made me feel guilty and ashamed for needing to know my children's genetic status," Mrs. Williams told [a congressional] hearing. . . .

Tonia Phillips had a hysterectomy and prophylactic mastectomy when she learnt that she was carrying the BRCA1 breast cancer susceptibility gene. As a result, the health care premiums for the small company she worked for were increased and she was asked to change insurance companies. She did not want to do this and eventually all employees had to pay half of their insurance premiums. "It seems unfair to me that I am taking steps to keep myself healthy and to prevent cancer in the future, and I am being singled out and made to feel I am a liability," she said.

GeneWatch UK,
"Genetic Discrimination by Insurers and Employers:
Still Looming on the Horizon," February 2006.

A number of states have passed state laws that prohibit certain forms of genetic discrimination. These laws, however, vary widely in the scope of their protection. Many are narrowly targeted to particular genetic conditions, some prohibit only certain types of screening but do not prohibit adverse employment actions based on genetic information, and some only address genetic counseling and confidentiality. These laws have been described as "a patchwork of provisions which are incomplete, even inconsistent, and which fail to follow a coherent vision for genetic screening, counseling, treatment and prevention of discrimination." In light of the inadequacies of federal and state law to address genetic discrimination issues, comprehensive federal legislation that specifically addresses these issues is necessary. . . .

How Laws Should Address Insurance Discrimination

Any proposed legislation should contain comprehensive protection against genetic discrimination by providers of health, life, disability, and other types of insurance. Legislation must bar insurers from making decisions about enrollment based on genetic information. It must also prohibit insurers from using genetic information in determining premium or contribution rates, or other terms or conditions of coverage. Finally, it must bar insurers from requesting or requiring an individual to undergo genetic testing.

Any proposed legislation must prohibit insurers from requiring, requesting, collecting, or buying genetic information about individuals who are covered or seeking coverage.

Insurers should be permitted, however, to obtain this information only for the limited purpose of paying for claims for genetic testing or other genetic services. Strict protections must be in place to ensure that when such information is requested, it is not used to affect an individual's enrollment, premiums, or terms or benefits of coverage.

Insurers must also be prohibited from disclosing genetic information to health plans or issuers of health insurance (except in the limited circumstances described above where the information is used for purposes of payment of claims), employers, and entities that collect and disseminate insurance information. . . .

Any proposed legislation must prohibit health care providers from requiring, requesting, or collecting genetic information about individuals who are seeking treatment. Providers may only collect this information for the purpose of providing genetic testing or other genetic services. Health care providers must not be permitted to disclose genetic information except to the patient, to insurers only for the limited purpose of seeking payment for genetic testing or genetic services rendered, to officials enforcing this legislation, or as required by other federal laws.

Periodical Bibliography

The following articles have been selected to supplement the diverse views presented in this chapter.

Laura B. Benko	"Genetic Conflict," *Modern Healthcare*, April 2, 2007.
Marie Cannizzaro	"3 Spinning Gold from the Double Helix," *Business*, June 2007.
Economist	"Storm in a Test Tube: Health Care," June 2, 2007.
Matthew Herper and Robert Langreth	"Will You Get Cancer?" *Forbes*, June 18, 2007.
Peter W. Huber	"MyGenes," *Forbes*, May 7, 2007.
Timothy F. Kim	"Newborn Exams May Soon Include DNA Screening," *Family Practice News*, June 1, 2000.
Newsweek	"Peering into the Future," December 11, 2006.
Steve Olson	"Who's Your Daddy? The Unintended Consequences of Genetic Screening for Disease," *Atlantic Monthly*, July–August 2007.
Don Romesburg	"May 27, 1997: Genetically Gay?" *Advocate*, July 17, 2001.
Alexandra Shimo	"A Diet Designed for Your Genes," *Maclean's*, June 11, 2007.
Nancy Shute	"Unraveling Your DNA's Secrets," *U.S. News & World Report*, January 8, 2007.
Emily Singer	"Choosing Babies," *Technology Review*, March–April 2007.
Gregory J. Tsongalis	"Genetic Testing: Current and Future Trends," *Medical Laboratory Observer*, October 2006.
Chantelle M. Wolpert	"Genetic Testing: Understanding the Basics," *JAAPA*, January 2005.

For Further Discussion

Chapter 1

1. In this chapter, what defines the beginning of human life for each author? How does that support the arguments for or against stem cell research? To which theory of life's beginning do you ascribe?

2. After reading the viewpoints in Chapter 1, consider to what degree governments should regulate scientific research. If not government, then who should make ethical decisions about research and medical practices that may impact an entire society?

Chapter 2

1. In the context of decision-making about human cloning, are religion and science always at odds? Find examples from the viewpoints to show instances of agreement and occasions of conflict.

2. According to Michael J. Sandel, what is at stake when people are allowed to select their offspring? How might the human race benefit from genetic engineering? Do the possible dangers outweigh the possible advantages, or visa versa?

Chapter 3

1. After reading the viewpoints in Chapter 3, try to determine what different authors believe about the relationship between the human body and what it means to be a person. Do you believe a person's essence is indistinguishable from the human body? Do you believe in the concept of a human soul or spirit?

2. The viewpoint by Cindy A. Smetanka and David K.C. Cooper and the viewpoint by Laura Purdy address animal-to-human organ transplantation. How do the authors distinguish between animals and human beings? What implications does the mixing of animal and human body parts have for definitions of what it means to be human?

Chapter 4

1. After reading the first two viewpoints in this chapter, consider why fetal genetic testing is more controversial for some people than adult genetic testing. Do you believe any of the uses of fetal genetic testing are justified or beneficial? Which uses do you find to be unethical?

2. Divide a piece of paper in half and make "pro" and "con" columns for each of these categories: immigration, the workplace, insurance. Write down the reasons different authors in this chapter are either for or against genetic testing in each category. Are there significant similarities in arguments against genetic testing? In arguments for genetic testing? Are there marked differences?

Organizations to Contact

The editors have compiled the following list of organizations concerned with the issues debated in this book. The descriptions are derived from materials provided by the organizations. All have publications or information available for interested readers. The list was compiled on the date of publication of the present volume; names, addresses, phone and fax numbers, and e-mail and Internet addresses may change. Be aware that many organizations take several weeks or longer to respond to inquiries, so allow as much time as possible.

American Medical Association (AMA)
515 N. State St., Chicago, IL   60610
(800) 621-8335
Web site: www.ama-assn.org

The AMA is the United States' largest professional organization for medical doctors. It helps set standards for medical practices and is a powerful lobby for physicians' interests. In order to address tough issues in medical ethics, the AMA includes an Institute for Ethics that establishes ethics policies to guide practicing physicians. It also develops educational programs that inform physicians on the means to address ethical and professional challenges. The association publishes several journals, including the monthly *Archives of Surgery*, and the weekly *JAMA*.

American Society of Law, Medicine, and Ethics (ASLME)
765 Commonwealth Ave., Suite 1634, Boston, MA   02215
(617) 262-4990
e-mail: info@aslme.org
Web site: www.aslme.org

The ASLME works to provide high-quality scholarship, debate, and critical thought to professionals concerned with ethical, legal, and social implications of healthcare dilemmas. It publishes the *Journal of Law, Medicine and Ethics* and a quarterly newsletter.

Canadian Bioethics Society

561 Rocky Ridge Bay NW, Calgary, AL   T2G 4E7
  Canada
(403) 208-8027
e-mail: lmriddell@shaw.ca
Web site: www.bioethics.ca

The Canadian Bioethics Society is an organization of both individuals and organizations from a wide variety of fields, including medicine, law, theology, philosophy, and public health, sharing common interests in ethical debates and in the human dimensions of health research and practice. The society publishes a twice-yearly newsletter.

Center for Bioethics

University of Pennsylvania, Philadelphia, PA   19104
(215) 898-7136 • fax: (215) 573-3036
Web site: www.bioethics.upenn.edu

The Center for Bioethics at the University of Pennsylvania runs the largest bioethics Web site and focuses on the ethical, efficient, and compassionate practice of the life sciences and medicine. The center publishes a newsletter, *PennBioethics*, twice a year.

Center for Responsible Genetics (CRG)

5 Upland Rd., Suite 3, Cambridge, MA   02140
(617) 868-0870
e-mail: crg@gene-watch.org
Web site: www.gene-watch.org

The CRG is a nonprofit group whose goal is to foster public debate about the social, ethical, and environmental implications of genetic technologies. CRG works through the media and concerned citizens to distribute accurate information and represent the public interest on emerging issues in biotechnology. CRG also publishes a bimonthly magazine, *GeneWatch*.

Centers for Disease Control and Prevention (CDC)
Division of Reproductive Health, Atlanta, GA   30341-3717
(770) 488-5200
Web site: www.cdc.gov/reproductivehealth

The CDC's Division of Reproductive Health provides informational reports on reproductive technologies; supports national and state-based surveillance systems to monitor trends and investigate health issues; conducts epidemiologic, behavioral, demographic, and health-services research; and works with partners to translate research findings into healthcare practice, public-health policy, and health-promotion strategies. The division provides all of its reports free of charge directly through its Web site.

The Christian Medical Fellowship (CMF)
6 Marshalsea Road, London   SE1 1HL
   United Kingdom
+44 (0)20 7234 9660
Web site: www.cmf.org.uk

The CMF is an organization that provides a Christian perspective on biomedical ethics issues. The CMF Works to support Christian doctors, medical students, and other healthcare professionals. It publishes numerous journals and articles on biomedical issues.

Euthanasia Research and Guidance Organization (ERGO)
24289 Norris Lane, Junction City, OR   97448-9559
(541) 998-1873
e-mail: ergo@efn.org
Web site: www.finalexit.org

The ERGO is a nonprofit educational corporation that believes voluntary euthanasia, physician-assisted suicide, assisted suicide, and self-deliverance are all appropriate life endings depending on the individual medical and ethical circumstances. The organization was founded in 1993, and its stated goal is to improve the quality of background research of assisted dying for persons who are terminally or hopelessly ill and wish to end their suffering. ERGO develops and publishes guidelines about life-ending decisions and offers many articles and books for purchase on their Web site.

The Hastings Center
21 Malcolm Gordon Rd., Garrison, NY   10524-4125
(845) 424-4040 • fax: (845) 424-4545
e-mail: mail@thehastingscenter.org
Web site: www.thehastingscenter.org

The Hastings Center is an independent, nonpartisan, and nonprofit bioethics research institute that is devoted to exploring the medical, ethical, and social implications of advances in healthcare, biotechnology, and the environment. Its publications include the *Hastings Center Report*.

Kennedy Institute of Ethics
Healy, 4th Floor, Georgetown University
Washington, DC   20057
(202) 687-8099 • fax: (202) 687-8089
Web site: http://Kennedyinstitute.georgetown.edu

The Kennedy Institute of Ethics supports medical ethics research on a variety of topics. It supplies the National Library of Medicine with an online bioethics database and publishes reports and articles on many medical ethics topics.

President's Council on Bioethics
1801 Pennsylvania Ave. NW, Suite 700
Washington, DC   20006
(202) 296-4669
e-mail: info@bioethics.gov
Web site: www.bioethics.gov

Since 2001, the President's Council on Bioethics has had the role of advising the president on bioethical issues that may emerge as a consequence of advances in biomedical science and technology. Publications by the council include *Reproduction and Responsibility* and *Human Cloning and Human Dignity.*

Treuman Katz Center for Pediatric Bioethics
PO Box 5371/71-1, Seattle, WA   98105
(206) 987-2000
e-mail: pcrc@seattlechildrens.org
Web site: http://bioethics.seattlechildrens.org

The Treuman Katz Center for Pediatric Bioethics is the nation's first bioethics center focused solely on pediatric issues. The center's goal is to create a permanent forum for national debate on the ethical issues that pediatric providers and researchers face each day. In order to educate healthcare professionals and foster debate, the center holds annual pediatric bioethics conferences.

Bibliography of Books

Swasti
Bhattacharyya

Magical Progeny, Modern Technology: A Hindu Bioethics of Assisted Reproductive Technology. Albany: State University of New York Press, 2006.

Edwin Black

War Against the Weak: Eugenics and America's Campaign to Create a Master Race. New York: Thunder Mouth Press, 2004.

Jess Buxton

The Rough Guide to Genes & Cloning. New York: Rough Guides, 2007.

Judith Daar

Reproductive Technologies and the Law. Newark, NJ: LexisNexis, 2006.

Celia Deane-
Drummond

Genetics and Christian Ethics. Cambridge, UK: Cambridge University Press, 2006.

Nancy Ehrenreich

The Reproductive Rights Reader. New York: New York University Press, 2007.

James H. Fetzer

Render Unto Darwin: Philosophical Aspects of the Christian Right's Crusade Against Science. Chicago: Open Court, 2007.

Cynthia Fox

Cell of Cells: The Global Race to Capture and Control the Stem Cell. New York: Norton, 2007.

Sarah Franklin

Dolly Mixtures: The Remaking of Genealogy. Durham, NC: Duke University Press, 2007.

Robin Marantz Henig — *Pandora's Baby: How the First Test Tube Babies Sparked the Reproductive Revolution.* Cold Spring Harbor, NY: Cold Spring Harbor Laboratory Press, 2006.

Bruce R. Korf — *Human Genetics and Genomics.* Malden, MA: Blackwell, 2007.

James V. Lavery — *Ethical Issues in International Biomedical Research: A Casebook.* New York: Oxford University Press, 2007.

Carol Levine — *Clashing Views on Controversial Bioethical Issues.* Guilford, CT: McGraw Hill, 2006.

Ricki Lewis — *Human Genetics: Concepts and Applications.* Boston: McGraw-Hill, 2007.

Alan Marzilli — *Stem Cell Research and Cloning.* New York: Chelsea House, 2007.

John F. Morris — *Medicine, Health Care, & Ethics: Catholic Voices.* Washington, DC: Catholic University of America Press, 2007.

Liza Mundy — *Everything Conceivable: How Assisted Reproduction Is Changing Men, Women, and the World.* New York: Knopf, 2007.

Peggy Orenstein — *Waiting for Daisy: A Tale of Two Continents, Three Religion, Five Infertility Doctors, An Oscar, An Atomic Bomb, a Romantic Night, and One Woman's Quest to Become a Mother.* New York: Bloomsbury USA, 2007.

Christopher Thomas Scott

Stem Cell Now: A Brief Introduction to the Coming Medical Revolution. New York: Plume, 2006.

Thomas A. Shannon

Genetics: Science, Ethics, and Public Policy: A Reader. Lanham, MD: Rowman & Littlefield, 2005.

Francoise Shenfield and Claude Surea

Contemporary Ethical Dilemmas in Assisted Reproduction. Abingdon: Informa Healthcare, 2006.

Debora L. Spar

The Baby Business: Elite Eggs, Designer Genes, and the Thriving Commerce of Conception. Boston: Harvard Business School Press, 2006.

J.R. Spencer and Antje de Bois-Pedain

Freedom and Responsibility in Reproductive Choice. Portland, OR: Hart, 2006.

David Wasserman, Jerome Bickenbach, and Robert Wachbroit

Quality of Life and Human Difference: Genetic Testing, Healthcare, and Disability. New York: Cambridge University Press, 2005.

Darrell M. West

Biotechnology Policy Across National Boundaries: The Science-Industrial Complex. New York: Palgrave Macmillan, 2007.

Barbara Wexler

Genetics and Genetic Engineering. Detroit, MI: Thomson Gale, 2004.

Index